ChatGPT for Beginners
Made Easy

Learn the Basics, Master Prompts, Boost
Productivity, and Cash In with Conversational AI

ModernMind Publications

Contents

Unlock Your Exclusive Bonus: 200+ Essential ChatGPT Prompts!

As a valued reader of "ChatGPT for Beginners Made Easy," you're entitled to a special gift that will supercharge your journey with ChatGPT—**a FREE collection of over 200 ChatGPT prompts** crafted to boost your productivity, streamline your tasks, and open new avenues for income.

Why This Bonus?

- **Maximize Efficiency**: Leverage these prompts to make ChatGPT your ultimate productivity partner.
- **Time-Saving Tips**: Cut down on trial and error with our expertly crafted queries.
- **Economic Opportunities**: Explore creative and practical ways to monetize your new skills.

Elevate your ChatGPT experience with this curated bonus. Whether you're looking to optimize your workflow, save valuable time, or explore new financial opportunities, these prompts are your first step towards achieving more with generative AI.

Get the bonus by scanning the QR code below.

Introduction

Imagine a personal assistant who could write articles and emails for you, quickly teach you new skills, create marketing material, and even help you start and run a business. Perhaps all on the same day. This assistant is always available and helps simplify your life by tracking your goals, organizing your to-do list, and helping you remember the highest priority items. Oh, and it doesn't cost you anything. Sounds like a game-changer, right?

Well, this "assistant" is a tool that already exists, and it's called ChatGPT. It's not something out of a sci-fi book. It's not simply a chatbot but rather an entry point into the exciting field of artificial intelligence. By picking up this book, you have taken the first step in understanding and using ChatGPT to its full potential.

Who Am I?

The same curiosity that brought you to ChatGPT also sparked my interest. I still clearly remember my first interaction with ChatGPT. It was like meeting an objective and highly knowledgeable partner eager to help me with whatever I needed.

As I have improved my skills and knowledge, ChatGPT has become an essential asset in both my personal and professional life. Utilizing this tool has significantly increased my productivity and transformed my approach to various tasks. What used to take me hours or even days is now completed in less than an hour, thanks to the efficiency and adaptability of ChatGPT. Its user-friendly interface and robust capabilities are now integrated into my daily routine, streamlining my workflow and freeing up valuable time. This newfound efficiency has not only enhanced the strategic elements of my business and career but also opened doors to multiple, mostly passive income streams, positively impacting my financial situation. The skills I have developed with ChatGPT enable me to capitalize on opportunities swiftly and effectively, ensuring that I stay ahead in a fast-evolving professional environment.

In short, my time spent with ChatGPT goes far beyond that of a simple user; it has become a vital resource that helps me accomplish tasks more quickly and profitably than ever before. Its impact on my life made me realize how much I wanted to share with newcomers to ChatGPT how to make the most of the platform.

I have seen the faces of friends, coworkers, and clients light up when they realize the possibilities of ChatGPT after I have shared my expertise and experiences with them. As part of that effort, this book will give you the tools to use ChatGPT effectively and accomplish your goals. I'm excited to take you on this same journey if that's what you choose.

Why This Book?

This book is your gateway to mastering ChatGPT, designed to ignite your excitement and prepare you for an exploration into the world of AI. Here's what sets this book apart:

Tailored for Beginners: Perfect for those new to AI, this guide demystifies complex concepts, offering clear, easy-to-follow explanations.

You'll find yourself swiftly moving from basic understanding to practical application, ready to use ChatGPT with confidence.

Hands On Learning Experience: Stand out with a book that focuses on real-world applications of ChatGPT and AI. Dive into case studies and interactive exercises that empower you to apply your newfound knowledge instantly. Encounter common challenges and learn strategic solutions to apply ChatGPT effectively in your daily tasks, ensuring you can immediately leverage your insights in a professional setting.

Current and Comprehensive: Stay ahead of the curve with the latest insights into the evolving world of ChatGPT. This book provides the freshest, most relevant content, ensuring you're well-equipped with the knowledge to excel in the field of artificial intelligence.

Whether you're enhancing your current career, kickstarting a lucrative venture, or boosting your productivity, this book is crafted for you. It's designed for both novices and those already familiar with ChatGPT, aiming to elevate your skills and enable you to harness the full power of this transformative technology. Discover how to craft effective prompts, increase your efficiency, and uncover the immense potential of ChatGPT in various professional scenarios.

My Commitment to Value

While it's possible to quickly generate content with AI, producing a book that's merely a collection of redundant, superficial content riddled with errors (you can find them in any niche), I chose a different path. This book was crafted with the assistance of AI, yet what elevates it is the human touch—my dedication to delivering genuine value to you, the reader.In the arena of AI-assisted writing, the distinction between a low-quality and a high-quality book is not merely in the use of technology but in the intent and expertise of the human guiding it.

I have meticulously utilized AI not just as a tool for writing, but as a collaborator, ensuring that every piece of content is refined, practical, and insightful. My extensive experience and hands-on engagement with ChatGPT have been instrumental in shaping a resource that is both informative and transformative. This book embodies a commitment to quality, leveraging the best of AI while infusing the care, understanding, and expertise that only a human can provide.

The difference lies in the commitment to excellence and the passion for empowering readers with knowledge that can genuinely make a difference in their lives. My aim is to present a book that not only harnesses the capabilities of AI but also reflects a deep commitment to providing real, tangible value, underscoring the transformative power of combining human insight with advanced technology. It also demonstrates to you, the reader, what's possible for you with ChatGPT and AI if you choose to develop your skills.

So, are you ready to learn a potentially life-changing skill? Settle in with your computer to your favorite chair, and let's unlock the incredible potential of ChatGPT together. Prepare to be amazed at how this technology can revolutionize your productivity, creativity, and problem-solving skills in no time.

Chapter 1

Dipping Your Toes into the AI Pond: A Beginner's Guide to ChatGPT

Are you interested in the mysterious world of AI and want to know how ChatGPT can help you? In this chapter, we will explore the fundamentals of ChatGPT without using complex terminologies that only computer scientists can understand, as well as what we can utilize ChatGPT for. My aim is to provide you with a basic understanding of AI and ChatGPT so that you can navigate this field with confidence going forward.

We will dive deeper into the basics of AI in this guide, and you don't need a Ph.D. to follow along. I understand that the world of AI can be overwhelming, but I'm here to help you make sense of it all.

By the end of this chapter, you will have a solid foundation of AI and a framework for your future success in ChatGPT. This guide will make traversing the world of AI feel like a leisurely stroll, not a frantic dash. I'm excited to take you on this adventure and introduce you to the future.

Understanding Artificial Intelligence: More than Just Sci-Fi

Artificial intelligence is no longer a concept reserved for science fiction movies. In fact, it is currently transforming the real world as we know it. AI refers to the programming of computers to learn and reason like humans, allowing machines to adapt, change, and grow similarly to humans.

AI has become an integral part of our lives and is often present in the background without us even noticing. For example, virtual assistants like Alexa or Google Assistant can play music or check the weather seamlessly, thanks to AI. The use of AI has allowed our smartphones to become intuitive and perform complex tasks beyond their traditional functionalities. That facial recognition feature you use to open your iPhone? That's AI. Predictive text? AI. You're likely already using AI every day, maybe without even realizing it.

The global market for AI is rapidly expanding, with an estimated annual growth rate of 17.3% between 2018 and 2030, and a market value predicted to reach $738.8 billion (Statista, n.d.). Major tech companies are investing heavily in AI research and development, as they recognize the significant impact it will have on our future. Additionally, new AI startups are popping up all over the place each and every day. It is clear that AI is no longer a distant concept, but is already present and changing our world.

The Brain Behind ChatGPT: Language Models

Ever wondered how ChatGPT engages in conversation so adeptly? Its proficiency stems from sophisticated language models, the core of its ability to comprehend and produce responses that mimic human interaction. These models delve into enormous text datasets, learning human language intricacies similarly to our own learning process involving grammar, syntax, and idioms.

Rather than simply memorizing text, these models employ advanced algorithms to predict words fitting the conversational context. For instance, mentioning "I feel like eating..." might prompt ChatGPT to suggest "pizza," reflecting its understanding of typical human preferences. This capability elevates ChatGPT from a basic chatbot to a master of dialogue, capable of delivering responses that are both appropriate and contextually relevant.

Decoding ChatGPT

ChatGPT transcends the conventional chatbot framework, distinguished by its dynamic range and depth of conversation. Developed by OpenAI, this tool leverages machine learning to craft responses that can be astonishingly human-like, offering versatility whether you're crafting an essay, seeking answers, or indulging in creative writing.

What is machine learning? Imagine teaching your dog new tricks, but instead of a dog, you have a computer. You show it lots of examples, like pictures of cats and dogs, and each time, you tell it which ones are cats and which ones are dogs. The computer looks for patterns in the pictures that help it figure out the difference on its own. Over time, just like your dog learns to fetch, the computer learns to correctly identify whether a new picture is a cat or a dog. This process of teaching the computer to learn from examples and improve its ability to make decisions or predictions is the essence of machine learning.

ChatGPT does this same thing but with words. It continuously learns from extensive textual data online, grasping not just the facts but the subtleties of conversational tone and context. This learning process allows ChatGPT to offer nuanced and informed interactions far beyond the capabilities of standard chatbots.

ChatGPT doesn't have a database of specific documents and sources, however. It's more like a seasoned tourist taking in the sights and sounds of a new place without meticulously documenting every detail, rather than Sherlock Holmes conducting a mental inventory.

It's important to note also that ChatGPT guarantees that your personal information is safe within its system. Your personal information is protected until you choose to provide it during a chat.

As we explore ChatGPT further, we uncover a groundbreaking AI companion, reshaping our interactions and expectations of machine intelligence. It's an embodiment of innovation, leaving users in awe of its conversational prowess and versatility.

A Quick History of OpenAI and ChatGPT

OpenAI is a world-renowned artificial intelligence research lab that has pioneered the creation of innovative tools like ChatGPT. Elon Musk, associated with OpenAI's inception, has influenced the foundational design of ChatGPT, reflecting his visionary approach to technology. However, ChatGPT isn't just a mimic; it's a dynamic entity, designed to push the boundaries of conventional AI applications, embodying OpenAI's ambition for a system that's both inventive and intuitive.

In order to trace the origins of ChatGPT, we need to go back to December 2015 when OpenAI was founded. OpenAI was not like any other tech startup, as it was created by a group of industry experts, including Sam Altman, Greg Brockman, Elon Musk, Ilya Sutskever, Wojciech Zaremba, and John Schulman (Marr, 2023). They were all digital entrepreneurs, machine learning specialists, and software developers who aimed to make artificial intelligence more useful to people.

On November 30, 2022, OpenAI unveiled ChatGPT to the world. Within a short period of time, it gained immense popularity worldwide for its incredible capabilities. People were amazed by how it could arrange perfect holidays, write captivating stories, and even generate code. In just five days, the platform went viral and attracted over a million users. Fast forward to the end of 2023, and OpenAI's revenue hit $1.6 billion annually, with a valuation of $86 billion, as reported by Deutscher in January 2024.

OpenAI has become a prominent organization thanks to careful planning and wise investments aimed at expanding the boundaries of artificial intelligence. In January 2023, Microsoft announced a multibillion-dollar investment to accelerate AI breakthroughs worldwide, solidifying its commitment to OpenAI. This expanded partnership reflects a mutual belief in OpenAI's ability to play a pivotal role in shaping the future of AI.

What Can ChatGPT Be Used For?

Next, we'll explore how ChatGPT surpasses mere conversation, unlocking new learning opportunities and providing insights that can revolutionize your daily life and learning experiences. Our exploration is aimed at demystifying how AI, particularly ChatGPT, is advancing and becoming an invaluable asset for everyday tasks and personal growth.

Think of ChatGPT as a multifunctional tool akin to a Swiss Army knife for intellectual exploration. It's designed to not only enhance your professional abilities but also to offer personal insights, helping you on your path to greater self-awareness. ChatGPT goes beyond generating text; it can transform the way you approach writing and communication, serving as your ally in reaching new creative or professional heights.

Utilizing ChatGPT doesn't require technical expertise. It's user-friendly and crafted to ensure that anyone, regardless of their familiarity with technology, can benefit from its capabilities. Its intuitive design simplifies the complex, making sophisticated technology accessible to all who are comfortable with basic digital tools.

In practical applications like customer service, ChatGPT proves invaluable, offering quick, efficient responses that can elevate a customer's experience with a brand. It stands as a steadfast support, streamlining interactions and delivering prompt solutions.

ChatGPT is not just another ordinary software; it acts as a catalyst for innovation by combining practicality with endless possibilities for both creative and routine tasks. In this section, we will explore some of its practical uses. The upcoming chapters will delve into a more comprehensive discussion of these features, including interactive exercises so you can try them for yourself.

Virtual Assistant: Simplifying Daily Tasks

Imagine having a personal assistant who is always ready to organize your schedule, manage your emails, and remind you of important dates. ChatGPT can embody this role perfectly, providing a seamless way to navigate your daily tasks with ease. It stands out not only for its ability to handle routine chores but also for making your day more manageable, allowing you to focus on what really matters.

Research Assistant: Streamlining Information Gathering

ChatGPT is an excellent digital research assistant that helps you dive into complex topics or quickly grasp summaries with ease. It can condense a large amount of information into easily understandable overviews without losing depth. This feature is invaluable for people who are short on time or need to learn the essentials of a subject quickly.

Writing Companion: Unleashing Creativity

ChatGPT assists in brainstorming, offers inspiration, and adds a unique twist to your writing projects. Whether you're crafting stories or exploring ideas, ChatGPT is by your side, encouraging your creative pursuits.

Boosting Personal Productivity

Task Management: ChatGPT is an excellent tool for keeping track of your tasks and revolutionizing the way you manage your to-do list. It helps you prioritize your duties and ensures that you don't miss anything important, replacing the clutter of paper or digital notes with a streamlined approach to task management.

Reminders: With ChatGPT, you can forget about missing important appointments or special occasions. It acts as a reliable reminder service, simplifying the process of setting reminders for everything from work meetings to personal events, ensuring that you're always on top of your schedule.

ChatGPT as a Personal Tutor

ChatGPT can also function as your personal tutor. With ChatGPT, you can have a reliable companion on your learning journey, whether you want to explore the world or become an expert in a particular field.

If you're interested in expanding your knowledge, ChatGPT can help you in an engaging and enjoyable way. You can ask anything, and ChatGPT will provide you with its extensive knowledge base, including informative summaries on different topics and explanations of complex concepts.

Moreover, if you're learning a new language, ChatGPT can be your language partner. It is not just another language textbook, but a real-world language helper. It can provide quick translations and even practice conversations in Spanish or French to improve your conversational skills.

ChatGPT as a Personal Writer

If you struggle with productivity, ChatGPT can be your personal writing assistant. It can help you communicate better and express yourself more effectively. Whether you need help drafting emails or creating social media posts and blog content, ChatGPT is your reliable partner.

One of the biggest challenges with email is knowing what to say and how to say it. ChatGPT can help you overcome writer's block and compose the perfect message, whether it's for business or personal purposes.

Blogging and social media require creativity and clarity. ChatGPT can help you produce engaging content quickly and efficiently. If you're struggling to come up with ideas or don't know where to start, ChatGPT can guide you through the writing process and make it easier for you to express yourself.

ChatGPT for Writer's Block

ChatGPT is a content producer that goes beyond the capabilities of traditional word processors. It can help you draft, revise, and perfect various types of content. If you're struggling with writer's block, ChatGPT can assist you in overcoming it. It can become your constant companion in the creative process, ready to generate ideas whenever needed. Whether you need help with ideas for articles, blog posts or social media content, ChatGPT can help you get unstuck and keep your creative juices flowing.

It's important to write engaging and concise material that is free of errors and easy to comprehend. ChatGPT can be useful not only during the brainstorming phase but also during the editing and proofreading stages. It analyzes your writing in detail, making suggestions to enhance clarity, eliminate errors, and make your writing shine.

ChatGPT for Professional Success

ChatGPT is an effective team player that can change the way teams approach projects and work together. With ChatGPT, project management and team coordination can be improved, which lays the groundwork for future success.

Timely Project Management — From Assignment to Tracking:
Managing a project can be complicated, but with ChatGPT, it becomes easier. ChatGPT assists with tracking work, assigning roles, and managing project tasks so your team can focus on making progress and achieving goals instead of getting lost in charts.

Finding the Best Time for Every Meeting is Easy: Setting up meetings can sometimes be a hassle, but ChatGPT makes it easy. It can identify convenient times for everyone to get together and streamline the process, removing the need for endless back-and-forth emails and constant calendar checking. This ensures that meetings are optimized for efficiency and booked without any hassle.

ChatGPT for Customer Service Enhancement

For achieving professional success, ChatGPT goes beyond its role as a customer service agent and becomes your business's first line of defense against problems.

Customers often ask similar questions, and ChatGPT excels at answering the most popular ones. This means that customer service reps can focus on more complicated and detailed issues while ChatGPT answers frequently asked questions immediately. This speed makes customers happier and allows your team to use their skills where they're most needed.

ChatGPT serves as a two-way street between organizations and customers, making it essential for acquiring insights. It's more than just a question-and-answer service. It actively involves customers in discussions, which helps to glean valuable feedback that can be used to improve the company's strategy and processes. As a tool for measuring customer happiness and pinpointing problem areas, ChatGPT plays an integral role in the never-ending cycle of improvement.

Chapter Wrap-Up

As we conclude this chapter, you should have a strong understanding of the foundational aspects of AI and how ChatGPT is an innovative tool that offers solutions and boosts productivity in various fields.

We have seen how ChatGPT, with its advanced language models, can be used as an assistant, advisor, and creative partner, seamlessly adapting to a wide range of tasks and challenges. This exploration aims to inspire and demonstrate the potential of ChatGPT to transform everyday tasks, simplify complex problems, and unlock new possibilities for innovation and efficiency.

However, with great power comes great responsibility. As we move from capabilities to considerations, our next chapter will cover the critical aspects of limitations and ethical considerations surrounding ChatGPT. It is vital to understand that while ChatGPT is a powerful tool, it is not without its boundaries and ethical implications. The upcoming discussion will equip you with the knowledge to navigate these challenges, ensuring that your use of ChatGPT is both effective and responsible, aligned with the highest standards of ethical practice.

In the following chapter, we will examine the limitations inherent in the technology, the ethical dilemmas it may pose, and the best practices to mitigate these challenges. This conversation is essential for anyone looking to leverage ChatGPT, as it prepares you to use the technology wisely, ethically, and with a full understanding of its impact.

Chapter 2

Navigating the Labyrinth: Understanding the Limits and Ethical Considerations

As you integrate ChatGPT into your workflows and your life, it's important to be aware of its features as well as its constraints and the potential risks lurking in the background. This chapter will act as your guide as you navigate the intricate maze of ChatGPT, where possibilities converge with limitations and innovation meets ethics.

The importance of ethical considerations in AI cannot be overstated. This section aims to guide you, not to scare you, by shedding light on essential but lesser-known aspects. By the end of this guide, you'll have the ability to use that knowledge to your advantage while exploring ChatGPT. Tackling ChatGPT's complexities head-on will ensure that you always make well-informed decisions.

ChatGPT's Shortcomings

Even though ChatGPT is powerful, it also has flaws. Let's shed light on its weaknesses so that we have a realistic picture of what it can do.

Producing Wrong or Illogical Answers

While ChatGPT is a reliable assistant that can generate text resembling human writing, it is not a perfect source of information and may sometimes provide wrong or nonsensical answers. It is crucial for users to understand this flaw and to use ChatGPT's features carefully. One of the advantages of machine learning and large language models is that they get smarter and less error-prone as they process more data. Therefore, it's likely that the occurrence of wrong and nonsensical answers from ChatGPT will decrease over time.

Historical Hurdles

One clear example of ChatGPT's flaws is in how it handles comments about historical events. When asked about historical facts, ChatGPT might give you information that isn't based on correct historical records. This limitation shows how important it is to be careful when looking into the past, and users are encouraged to check information from different trusted sources to make sure it is correct.

Challenges in the Workplace

In a professional setting, precision is crucial, making it essential to recognize ChatGPT's limitations. Inaccurate or nonsensical responses from ChatGPT can result in misunderstandings or unsuccessful communications, potentially leading to significant repercussions in the workplace. Professionals utilizing ChatGPT must exercise caution, understand its boundaries, and strategically deploy it in situations where accuracy is imperative. It's vital to assess the context in which ChatGPT is used, ensuring it aligns with the need for precise and reliable information.

The Literal Machine and Creative Constraints

ChatGPT is very good at understanding language, but it often takes things literally. When used in artistic projects, this trait has its limits, even though it is helpful in other situations. When telling stories or thinking creatively, where freedom and creativity are fundamental, ChatGPT's tendency to be literal can be a problem.

It's essential for people who use ChatGPT for artistic tasks like writing stories to know that this machine, while intelligent, only does what it's programmed to do. It's very good at knowing what's happening and generating sensible responses. Still, its answers might not be as creative or unique as human minds.

Users should be careful when it comes to creative writing, where radical ideas and story twists are valued. ChatGPT can help improve and organize current ideas. Still, it might need help to generate new ideas beyond what is ordinarily possible. This is because it can't really think "outside the box," which is where human instincts and imagination usually rule.

Privacy Concerns About Data

Carefully managing personal info is one of the most important things to consider regarding AI interactions. As a matter of principle, OpenAI does not save any information that users enter into ChatGPT. This dedication to privacy provides a comforting basis, informing users that their contributions are neither stored nor used in any way apart from the current discourse.

Users must also be vigilant about the data they input into ChatGPT. Despite OpenAI's policy of not retaining user data, it's up to the users to safeguard their personal information. This responsibility sets the foundation for a secure and trustworthy relationship with AI technologies, ensuring user confidence.

Use Caution Around Private Data

The platform's data protection policy adds an extra layer of safety. As a machine, ChatGPT can't tell the difference between private and public details. Users play a crucial role by being cautious and reflective in their interactions, considering the potential consequences of the data they submit.

Staying Anonymous

In the context of data security, proactive measures are essential. Users are encouraged to take precautions and not provide personally identifiable information. This category includes information such as names, addresses, and credit card numbers. This kind of preventative action is in line with privacy best practices and helps foster an AI culture that is safe and trustworthy.

Find Your Way in the AI-Influenced Job Market

The growing concern that AI will replace human workers is a significant issue in AI research and development. There is a genuine fear that certain occupations may become automated with the increasing sophistication of AI. When a business decides to use ChatGPT to automate the production of its blog entries, an intriguing scenario arises. This scenario raises an important question: what happens to the human authors who wrote these in the first place? It's a complicated problem with many angles that will require serious thought from the public in the future.

But an important detail comes to light in this conversation: people will always need to lead from behind the scenes. ChatGPT is an example of AI, and while it has the potential to automate some tasks, human intelligence is still far superior. Knowing how to use and guide tools like ChatGPT correctly will be critical in the not-too-distant future workplace.

As we progress with automation and AI, we must remember that these technological advances will make us more productive and help the economy grow. However, with this development comes a potential difficulty: millions worldwide may need to switch careers or improve their skill sets. By 2030, automation may have forced the relocation or retraining of 400 million to 800 million individuals worldwide (Kolmar, 2023).

This seismic upheaval highlights the significance of proactive efforts. Successfully navigating the constantly shifting employment market will take a concerted group effort to encourage skill growth and ease job changes. Human adaptability and technical innovation must work in tandem to build a future where AI integration not only boosts productivity but also keeps the workforce resilient and prepared for tomorrow's problems.

The Dark Side of AI and the Ethical User

It's essential to keep our excitement in check when we're amazed by what AI can do by recognizing that it has two sides. As AI adoption grows, its dark side is already being exposed. ChatGPT's proficiency in producing natural-sounding writing makes it vulnerable to abuse for malicious reasons like creating deepfakes or spreading misinformation. Other AI tools that can produce video or speech are just as vulnerable. Taylor Swift and President Joe Biden have already fallen victim to AI deep fakes, demonstrating that these acts can have real-world consequences for everyone. There will be a lot of money to be made in the future by companies that can effectively and reliably identify and shut down deep fake content.

In the meantime, awareness and duty are vital, and the fact that someone could use ChatGPT for fraudulent purposes shows how important they are. Users, creators, and the general public should understand the ethical duties of using AI tools. In this new world driven by AI, being alert to possible misuse becomes a shared duty. This creates a commitment to protecting the integrity of information.

It's not just about using the tool; it's about being conscious of the impact your usage can have and striving towards a future where AI enhances societal well-being. By making a concerted societal effort to use AI ethically, we may pave a way that optimizes advantages while limiting risks, creating a world where creativity and accountability coexist.

While ChatGPT is an advanced language model, it's not infallible or omniscient. Understanding its limitations simplifies the interaction, fostering a synergy where human intelligence amplifies AI's utility.

Stay Informed

Navigating the ethical landscape of AI is an ongoing endeavor, requiring users to stay informed about the latest in AI ethics and regulations. As AI technology and its societal implications evolve, so too should the user's approach to engaging with it, always aligning with the latest ethical standards and industry best practices.

In the collaborative venture of AI development, staying informed is crucial. An informed user is empowered, capable of navigating AI's complexities with confidence and contributing to the technology's ethical advancement. Through informed engagement, users can play a part in shaping a responsible AI framework that aligns with community values.

The commitment to responsible AI usage is a collective endeavor involving users, developers, and policymakers. It's about fostering a culture where ethical considerations are integral to AI development, ensuring that technology not only advances but does so in a way that reflects our shared values. By working together, we can embed ethical principles into the very core of AI innovation, making responsible use a universal standard.

Navigating Ethical Gray Zones

Ethical concerns arise as an essential part of the AI application environment, especially when using AI-powered content creation tools like ChatGPT.

Content Authorship Problem

When you think about who wrote material made with ChatGPT, you come up with an ethical contradiction. For instance, who should get the credit if ChatGPT was used to write a blog article? Does the AI create material based on the instructions given by a human being, or does the human only serve as a guide?

Problems with Attributing Authorship

A significant obstacle is sorting out the subtle differences between human input and AI-generated content. ChatGPT generates material while being guided by an individual's input on topic and context. It's essential to strike a balance when deciding who gets credit for what, as writing is often a group effort.

Accountability and Openness

For ethical reasons, there must be openness and responsibility. Users of ChatGPT who regularly produce content should have well-defined policies and standards in place governing who gets credit for what. Explaining how AI has worked together to create information improves clarity and reduces room for disagreement.

Chapter Wrap-Up

In concluding our exploration of the ethical considerations and limitations of ChatGPT, we've navigated the complex terrain where cutting-edge technology meets human values. This chapter has underscored the importance of approaching ChatGPT with a mindful awareness of its potential and its boundaries. As we've seen, while ChatGPT is a remarkable tool capable of transforming various aspects of our professional and personal lives, it carries with it responsibilities that we, as users, must diligently uphold.

Understanding the limitations of ChatGPT helps us set realistic expectations and use the AI more effectively, ensuring that we rely on its capabilities without overstepping into areas where its application could be problematic or ethically questionable. Moreover, the ethical framework we adopt in our interaction with ChatGPT is crucial—it not only guides our immediate use of the technology but also shapes its future development and integration into society.

As we move forward, let's carry with us the insights gained from this chapter, ensuring that our engagement with ChatGPT and similar AI technologies remains rooted in a commitment to ethical integrity, societal benefit, and mindful usage. The journey with AI is an ongoing one, and staying informed, conscious, and reflective about our interactions with such technologies will enable us to harness their power responsibly and innovatively.

Chapter 3

ChatGPT Essentials: Setup and First Steps

The possibilities are endless as you learn how to leverage ChatGPT, and this chapter is designed to guide you along the way. Here, we cover the details, providing a clear and comprehensive introduction to getting started with ChatGPT. This is where you can begin to fully explore the capabilities of this powerful AI tool.

When it comes to understanding what ChatGPT can do, the most important thing to bear in mind is that this chapter is here to help you start smoothly. Whether you are new to the world of artificial intelligence or have some experience, there are some basics you should know to get the most out of your interactions with ChatGPT.

Let's skip the small talk and get straight to the point. The steps in this chapter are like a roadmap, making it easy to follow along and ensure that you set up ChatGPT correctly. From accessing the tool to configuring it for optimal performance, this chapter demystifies the process so that you can use ChatGPT with confidence and get the most out of it.

Resources Required to Use ChatGPT

Having a reliable internet connection is crucial when it comes to exploring the features of ChatGPT. The quality of your experience with the AI is directly proportional to the speed and reliability of your internet connection. Just like a conductor leading a symphony orchestra, a fast internet connection ensures smooth and quick communication with the AI.

Additionally, the technology underpinning your ChatGPT interaction goes much beyond the digital umbilical cord of a steady internet connection. An adequately outfitted machine keeps that channel open for a more natural and effective exchange of information.

Stated more simply, having a fast internet connection and a decent computer or smartphone helps a lot.

Setting Up ChatGPT: How to Install

Once you've made your way across cyberspace to OpenAI's website, installing ChatGPT is a reassuringly simple process. To get access to ChatGPT, follow the instructions below:

Step 1: Navigating to the ChatGPT Website

Head on over to ChatGPT at chat.openai.com. The platform's website is again designed with the user in mind, making navigating and accessing all available data and tools simple.

Step 2: Begin the Registration Procedure

Find the part where you can register or sign up for the site. It's easy to get started with the signup procedure. Clicking the "Sign Up" button will navigate you to a signup sheet. Include your email address and a strong password when prompted to do so.

Step 3: Email Verification

After completing the registration form, OpenAI will send a confirmation email to the address you gave. Look in your mailbox for a verification email, then use its instructions to confirm your account. This is an essential part of setting up your account safely and quickly. Once you verify your email, make sure you can get logged in.

If you're having trouble, please see the Appendix in the back of this book to troubleshoot some common setup issues.

Step 4: Subscription Plans (Optional)

Check out OpenAI's subscription options to see what fits your needs. Although there may be no cost to use the service, a paid subscription may be worth it to unlock extra services and increase your data use cap. Choose a plan that corresponds with your requirements and preferences.

Step 5: Testing ChatGPT

Now that everything is all set up, it's time to have your first conversation with the tool.

How can I help you today?

Compare design principles
for mobile apps and desktop software

Plan a trip
to see the northern lights in Norway

Brainstorm names
for my fantasy football team with a frog theme

Design a database schema
for an online merch store

Message ChatGPT...

Upon logging into the tool, you'll see on your screen, "How Can I Help You Today?"

Below that there are several boxes that have suggestions for prompts. You can click one of them to see ChatGPT in action. Go ahead, try it.

Additionally, you will see what looks similar to a Google search bar towards the bottom of the page. Here, you can ask ChatGPT anything. You can start by giving it a prompt such as:

"Which is the best dog breed for apartment living?"

The response will start a conversation so you can continue to know more about such breeds. Once ChatGPT is up and running, you can dive headfirst into discovering how AI may improve your life.

Remember that the documentation is there to help you as you use the platform to get the most out of it. Enjoy exploring!

Interactive Learning with ChatGPT

Explore the core of ChatGPT's features more interactively by starting in OpenAI's Playground. In this dynamic space, testing and learning come together. It's not just a tool; it's an exploratory canvas where you can see how different questions and prompts affect ChatGPT's responses in real-time.

OpenAI's Playground shows that anyone can learn ChatGPT. Unlike some more typical educational environments, this platform doesn't need any further configurations to start teaching. It's a safe refuge for newcomers and seasoned pros alike, providing an easy way to get started with interactive AI.

You can test ChatGPT's interpretation and response mechanisms to various questions within the safe bounds of the Playground. It goes beyond textbook knowledge to add a real-world perspective to your education. The responses you receive reveal ChatGPT's nuanced language comprehension, demonstrated in its more than simple answers.

The quick feedback loop provided by the Playground is what makes it so important. It's not just there to watch while you study; it actively participates in the process and reacts in real-time to the questions and challenges you provide. This fluid exchange of ideas turns your education into a two-way conversation with the AI, broadening your perspective and helping you better comprehend its potential.

The Playground is like having a helpful older sibling while you're just starting to work with ChatGPT. It invites you to hone your abilities without any danger to yourself. There's more to it than just the directions you type in. It's about learning, making changes, and seeing how ChatGPT changes as you improve.

In a nutshell, OpenAI's Playground is more than just a place to learn; it's also a place where theoretical concepts can be put into practice, where novices may find a resource that simplifies AI, and where curiosity can meet reality. Think of this place as more than simply a starting point; use it to launch an in-depth investigation of everything ChatGPT has to offer, turning abstract concepts into practically functional abilities as you go.

Exercise

Let's do a little hands-on work to promote collaborative learning. Make a basic question or statement that will allow you to enter the world of ChatGPT. Whatever it is—a question, a phrase, or a topic of interest—this hands-on experience goes beyond the theoretical and lets you see the AI's answer for yourself.

1. Ask a Question

Start by asking:

What do you know about *[Topic of Interest]*?

See how it responds with a detailed answer.

2. Ask a Follow-Up Question

You may then continue the conversation by asking:

What is the best way to learn "Topic of Interest"?

3. Ask it to Tailor It's Response for a Certain Audience

Then you can ask something like:

Explain to me in a tone that is more appropriate for 8th graders.

This hands-on exercise is more than a demonstration; it's an invitation to get involved with ChatGPT and turn theoretical principles into real-world insights.

If you're just getting started with this method, remember that it's not meant to replace the way you've always learned; instead, it's an innovative way to connect the dots between theory and practice. If you want to learn more about ChatGPT's language skills, you can use the Playground as more than just a place to watch. By asking questions, you can shape the learning experience, and each interaction takes you further along the path.

Cultivating Patience

Patience becomes a foundational virtue in technology education. Adding ChatGPT to your arsenal is a marathon, not a quick dash, and you must approach it as such. Problems and errors are not indications of insufficiency but rather necessary parts of the educational process.

Running into difficulties and working through subtleties that appear puzzling at first is typical. Remember what it was like learning how to tie your shoes or drive a car? You weren't good at it at first. Patience is a valuable asset, not just a virtue. Patience is the thread that holds your knowledge together, allowing you to untangle the knots of technology slowly.

Mastery does not suddenly become clear in a singular moment but develops over time. Each new challenge you overcome is evidence of your growing skill. This means that patience isn't just putting up with things; it's also taking part in the process. It's an acknowledgment that you'll only really understand ChatGPT once you face and overcome its many obstacles.

Remember that difficulties and slip-ups are par for the course while you travel this road. Don't let them stop you from pursuing your interest in technology; instead, use them as guides. When something goes wrong, you're not going backward; you're just changing your direction. You can transform your learning expedition from a haphazard, unfulfilling ordeal into a thoughtful, enjoyable, and eventually gratifying one if you practice patience and persevere through the complexities of ChatGPT's setup.

Chapter Wrap-Up

Before we move on to the next chapter, it's important to make sure that you have successfully logged in to ChatGPT. This is a critical step as it will enable you to fully participate in the interactive and exploratory learning experience that we will undertake together. Your ability to log in seamlessly is not only a milestone but also a key indicator of your readiness to engage deeply with ChatGPT's capabilities.

In the upcoming chapter, we will start navigating the challenges of prompt engineering. We will dive deep into the art and science of crafting effective prompts. This skill will enhance your interactions with ChatGPT and enable you to unleash its full potential. This foundational knowledge is vital to unlocking more sophisticated uses of the AI, making it possible for you to create, innovate, and solve problems with unparalleled efficiency.

So, take a moment to verify your successful login, and get ready for an exhilarating exploration of prompt engineering. Our next chapter will equip you with the knowledge and skills you need to communicate effectively with ChatGPT, setting the stage for a rewarding experience with this transformative technology.

Chapter 4
Creating Effective Prompts

How one interacts with conversational AI models such as ChatGPT can make a significant difference in the quality and utility of the AI's responses. The craft of prompt engineering extends beyond the simple act of questioning—it's about the finesse with which you phrase those questions. This chapter focuses on unwrapping the subtleties of creating prompts, arming you with the knowledge and techniques to improve your engagements with ChatGPT.

We will cover the essential strategies for those just starting out, pinpoint typical errors to steer clear of, and reveal more sophisticated methods for experienced users. Additionally, the chapter underscores the necessity of keeping current with ongoing developments in AI technology.

This chapter is an aid for anyone, whether they are newcomers to AI or seeking to polish their skills in prompt creation. We will cover a range of topics, from crafting straightforward inquiries to utilizing detailed instructions for more elaborate tasks. By the conclusion of this chapter, you'll possess the ability to design prompts that are not only potent but also finely tuned to your goals.

It's important to remember that the mastery of prompt engineering is an evolving discipline. As ChatGPT advances, your strategies should advance in tandem. This chapter will show you how to stay in step with these advancements, helping ensure your prompts continue to draw out the best in AI responses. Here, your words are the keystrokes that define the dialogue.

Sparking Conversation: The Basics of Writing Prompts

A prompt is essentially your way of starting a conversation—it's the input you provide, whether a question or a statement, to receive the information or assistance you're seeking. Let's dig into how to do this effectively.

Crafting Your Prompt

Imagine you're a chef about to prepare a meal—the ingredients you choose and how you combine them will determine the dish's outcome. Similarly, the prompt you craft is the recipe for the response you'll receive from ChatGPT.

For instance, if you're gearing up to use ChatGPT to assist with composing an email, the prompt might be structured as follows: "Draft an email to my team regarding the schedule for tomorrow's meeting, emphasizing the need for punctuality and the agenda items to be discussed."

Notice the specificity here—it's what makes the difference between a response that's a gourmet dish and one that's just a snack. A broad prompt like "Write something" is the culinary equivalent of throwing random ingredients into a pot and hoping for the best. Instead, you want to be the gourmet chef of your prompts.

Understanding Prompt Structure

The structure of a great prompt can usually be broken down into two key components: the instruction and the task.

1. **Instruction:** This tells ChatGPT what you want to do. It's the 'verb' in your sentence, your action command. For example, "Summarize", "Explain", "Translate", "Draft", etc.
2. **Task:** This specifies the subject or object of your instruction. It's the 'noun' or 'content' in your sentence that you want the action to be performed on.

To illustrate, in the prompt "Translate the following English text to French: 'Hello, how are you?'", "Translate the following English text to French:" is the instruction, and "'Hello, how are you?'" is the task.

Exercises for Practice

1. **Specificity Practice:** Take the general prompt "Write about a historical event" and refine it to be as specific as possible. For example, "Write a summary of the events leading up to the signing of the Declaration of Independence on July 4th, 1776, emphasizing the role of the Continental Congress."
2. **Prompt Dissection:** Look at the following prompt: "Create a list of exercises for a 30-minute high-intensity workout session for beginners." Identify the instruction and the task.
3. **Role Play:** Pretend you're using ChatGPT to help with different tasks, such as planning a trip, doing homework, or learning a new skill. Write three different prompts for these scenarios, focusing on being clear and specific.

Remember, the key to a successful interaction with ChatGPT is in how you frame your prompt. A well-crafted prompt leads to a precise, useful, and satisfying response, much like a well-followed recipe leads to a delicious meal. Now, let's turn these principles into practice and create prompts that will spark the best conversations with ChatGPT.

Prompting Productivity: Crafting Prompts for Specific Tasks

To harness the full potential of ChatGPT, tailoring your prompts to fit the particular task you're tackling is essential. This bespoke approach to prompt crafting ensures that the responses you receive are not just accurate but also practical and immediately applicable to your needs.

Prompt Customization for Task Efficiency

Just like a key is designed to fit a specific lock, your prompt should be designed to unlock the potential of ChatGPT for the task at hand.

- **Customer Service Optimization:** When you're fielding customer inquiries, precision in your prompts can make the difference. For example, a customer service prompt could be, "Draft a polite and informative response to a customer inquiring about our 30-day return policy, including the necessary steps they need to follow."
- **Content Creation Enhancement:** If you're leaning on ChatGPT for generating content, specificity will be your ally. A content creation prompt might read, "Compose a 500-word blog post on the environmental and economic benefits of adopting solar energy, targeted at homeowners."

The Art of Experimentation

Finding the right prompt is often a process of trial and error. Just as scientists experiment with different variables to achieve the best outcome, you should feel free to test various prompt styles.

- **Iterative Prompting:** Don't hesitate to refine your prompts. If the first response doesn't quite hit the mark, adjust your prompt for clarity, detail, or scope, and try again.
- **Precision Targeting:** Aim for clarity and specificity in your prompts. The goal is to provide enough direction to steer

ChatGPT toward the desired outcome without being overly prescriptive, which might limit the model's creative potential.

Exercises for Practice

1. **Prompt Refinement:** Start with a general prompt, like "Help me with customer service," and refine it step by step until it becomes a clear, actionable request. Reflect on how each change could affect the response from ChatGPT.
2. **Content Variation:** Write a series of prompts asking for a blog post about solar energy, each with a different angle or target audience. Compare how the subtle changes in the prompts can lead to significantly different articles.
3. **Feedback Loop:** Use ChatGPT to answer a prompt, then, based on the response, modify the prompt to get a more targeted answer. This exercise will help you understand how even small changes in wording can significantly alter the response.

By mastering the art of prompt crafting, you can transform your interactions with ChatGPT into a highly productive dialogue perfectly tailored to your specific tasks. Remember, the right prompt is the key to unlocking the full capabilities of ChatGPT, making your work more efficient and effective. If there's one thing to remember from this chapter, it's that prompt engineering is an art that only improves with a lot of repetition. Developing the knack for writing effective prompts for ChatGPT is akin to honing any other skill: it gets better with practice.

Avoiding Pitfalls: Common Mistakes in Writing Prompts

Familiarizing oneself with some common missteps and understanding how to avoid them can dramatically shorten the learning curve.

Navigating the Pitfalls of Prompt Construction

Just like a chef learns to balance flavors, the art of crafting prompts is about striking a balance between clarity and conciseness.

- **The Perils of Ambiguity:** A common error is crafting prompts that are too broad or nonspecific, which can lead to responses that are less than helpful. A prompt like "*Tell me about dogs*" casts too wide a net, garnering a generic response. Go ahead, try it. Contrastingly, "*Provide an overview of the average lifespan and prevalent health conditions in Golden Retrievers*" pinpoints the information needed, leading to a more tailored and informative response.
- **The Overload Conundrum:** Another slip-up is the temptation to pack a prompt with excessive information. Specificity is crucial, but an overload of details can muddy the waters, leading to a muddled response. A prompt like "*Draft a comprehensive article detailing the history, types, uses, and advantages of solar power across residential, commercial, and industrial sectors*" is ambitious but scattershot. It's more effective to segment the prompt into focused questions, such as "*Outline the history of solar energy*," followed by separate prompts for types, uses, and sector-specific benefits. I encourage you to see for yourself by entering these prompts into ChatGPT.

Practical Tips for Precise Prompts

Embrace Brevity

Aim to distill your prompt down to the essential information needed for the task. This approach ensures clarity without overwhelming the model. Let's say you're interested in learning how to bake sourdough bread and want to use ChatGPT to guide you through the process.

Initial Prompt with Multiple Details: "*Explain how to bake sourdough bread, including the preparation of the starter from scratch, the exact flour-to-water ratios for perfect hydration, the significance of ambient* *temperature, the folding technique versus kneading, how to know when the dough has fermented enough, the impact of different types of flour, the history of sourdough bread, and various ways to score the loaf before baking."*

Revised Balanced Prompt: *"Can you guide me through the basic steps of baking sourdough bread, focusing on preparing the starter, the dough fermentation process, and baking tips?"*

The revised prompt is succinct and focuses on the key aspects you want to learn about, making it clear but not overwhelming, and allowing ChatGPT to provide focused, actionable information.

Segment Complex Requests

If the topic is multifaceted, consider breaking it down into a series of prompts. This allows ChatGPT to address each aspect with the necessary depth and precision.

Avoid Double-Barreled Questions

Questions that ask for multiple pieces of information in one go can be tricky. It's often more effective to ask separate questions for each piece of information you're seeking.

Let's say you're interested in learning about the impact of climate change on global agriculture. This is a complex topic that can be segmented into several prompts to cover different aspects systematically. Here's how you might approach it:

1. Basic Understanding of Climate Change:

- *"Explain the basic scientific principles of climate change."*

2. Link Between Climate Change and Agriculture:

- *"How does climate change affect agricultural practices globally?"*

3. Specific Impacts on Agriculture:

- *"What are the specific effects of rising temperatures on crop yields?"*
- *"Describe how changes in precipitation patterns impact irrigation needs."*

4. Regional Differences:

- *"Compare the impact of climate change on agriculture in temperate vs. tropical regions."*

5. Adaptive Strategies for Farmers:

- *"What strategies are farmers using to adapt to climate change?"*

6. Technological Innovations:

- *"Discuss technological innovations that are helping agriculture adapt to climate change."*

7. Policy and Climate Change:

- *"What policies are being implemented to mitigate the impact of climate change on agriculture?"*

8. Future Projections:

- *"What are the projections for the impact of climate change on agriculture over the next 50 years?"*

By breaking down the broad topic into these focused prompts, you can systematically explore the subject and build a comprehensive understanding of how climate change is affecting global agriculture. Each prompt acts as a segment of the broader topic, and when combined, they provide a detailed overview.

Exercises for Refinement

1. **Vagueness Reduction:** Take a broad prompt and practice refining it to increase specificity. Notice how the responses change as the prompts become more focused.
2. **Information Balancing:** Write a prompt that includes multiple details, then revise it to find the sweet spot where you provide just enough information to be clear but not so much that it's confusing.
3. **Segmentation Strategy:** For a complex topic, create a series of prompts that collectively cover the entire subject. This helps you learn how to approach extensive topics systematically.

By sidestepping these common mistakes, you can craft prompts that are sharp and efficient, steering ChatGPT toward producing the most relevant and precise information in response to your queries. This doesn't just save time; it enhances the quality of the interaction, ensuring that you get exactly what you need from the model.

Mastering Prompts: Advanced Techniques for Effective Prompts

As your fluency with ChatGPT grows, you can begin to employ advanced techniques in your prompts that refine the outcome and open up new possibilities for interaction. These techniques can enhance the model's output, particularly for complex or creative tasks.

Chaining Prompts for Coherent Narratives

Chaining prompts is like creating a series of stepping stones that lead the model through a task. This approach is particularly useful for long-form writing or multi-step problems.

- **Narrative Construction:** For instance, when crafting a story, start with a foundational prompt: *"Begin a short story set on Mars with an unexpected discovery."* Once ChatGPT generates the opening paragraph, use its output to build the next prompt: *"Continue the story, focusing on the main character's reaction to the discovery."*
- **Iterative Development:** Each subsequent prompt leverages the preceding response, creating a cohesive and engaging narrative. This method is not limited to storytelling—it can also be applied to software development, lesson planning, or any task that benefits from a sequential build-up.

See It In Action

Let's take the example of lesson planning for a course on basic web development. The goal is to structure the course content using iterative prompts that build upon each other.

1. Course Outline Creation:

"Draft a high-level outline for a six-week web development course for beginners."

Assuming the output is a weekly breakdown of topics, we move to the next prompt based on this structure.

2. Week 1 Breakdown:

"Expand on the first week's topic of 'Introduction to HTML' by listing key concepts and skills that should be covered."

Based on the list of key concepts provided, we can continue to the next stage.

3. Lesson Plan for Day 1:

"Create a detailed lesson plan for the first day, focusing on 'The Structure of an HTML Page'."

Once you have the structure for Day 1, you can iterate further.

4. Interactive Elements:

"Based on the day 1 lesson plan, suggest interactive exercises that reinforce the understanding of HTML page structure."

After integrating exercises into Day 1, you can move on to subsequent days.

5. Subsequent Days' Focus:

"Given the structure and exercises for Day 1, propose topics and activities for Day 2 that introduce 'HTML Tags and Attributes'."

Continuing this process, you build up each day's lesson plan, each week's focus, and eventually the entire course.

6. Assessment and Feedback:

"For the end of Week 1, devise a simple project that tests the students' understanding of all HTML topics covered and provide guidelines for peer feedback."

This iterative process ensures that each step in lesson planning is thoughtful, coherent, and builds upon the previous steps, ultimately resulting in a well-structured course with clear learning objectives and engaging content.

System-Level Instructions for Refined Output

Incorporating system-level instructions into your prompts allows you to guide not just the content but also the tone, style, or format of ChatGPT's responses.

- **Tone Guidance:** For example, you might need to translate a message while maintaining a certain formality. A prompt such as *"Translate the following English text to French, maintaining a formal tone: 'Good morning, I hope this message finds you well,'"* instructs ChatGPT to keep the translation polite and professional.

- **Style Specification:** Similarly, if you're aiming for a particular writing style, such as persuasive or expository, you can direct ChatGPT accordingly: *"Write a persuasive introduction for an article advocating for renewable energy solutions."*

Exercises for Mastery

1. **Prompt Chaining Practice:** Write a series of chained prompts to guide ChatGPT through planning a small event. Start with the event concept and chain prompts to cover location, guest list, and agenda.
2. **System-Level Instruction Application:** Create prompts that specify different tones (e.g., friendly, authoritative, casual) and styles (e.g., persuasive, informative) for the same piece of content, and observe how the tone and style influence the final output.
3. **Format Direction:** Experiment with prompts that request responses in specific formats, such as a bulleted list, a dialogue, or a poem. For example: *"In the form of a poem, describe a sunset over the ocean."*

These advanced techniques can significantly boost the effectiveness of your prompts, giving you greater control over the complexity and quality of ChatGPT's responses. With practice, these methods will become a natural part of your prompt-crafting toolkit, allowing you to achieve nuanced and sophisticated results from your interactions with the model.

Staying Informed: Keeping up with Updates in Prompt Engineering

Staying current with the latest advancements in AI and ChatGPT is crucial. As ChatGPT advances, the strategies for crafting prompts evolve alongside it.

Continuous Learning for Improved Prompt Design

- **Adapting to Innovation:** With each iteration of ChatGPT, new features and refinements may alter how we approach prompt engineering. Keeping abreast of these updates ensures that you are using the most effective techniques.
- **Resource Utilization:** To stay informed, consider following the OpenAI blog, which provides official updates and insights. Joining online communities such as the ChatGPT subreddit or other forums dedicated to AI can also be invaluable. These platforms often share user experiences, troubleshooting, and creative uses of the technology that you may not find in official documentation.

Developing a Prompt Engineering Mindset

- **Stay Updated:** Schedule regular intervals to check for updates on ChatGPT and review the latest best practices for prompt engineering.
- **Engage with the Community:** Participate in discussions and share your experiences. The collective intelligence of a community can be a powerful tool for learning.
- **Iterative Learning:** Use feedback from your prompts to refine your approach continually. If a prompt doesn't yield the desired outcome, reframe it and try again.

- **Documentation:** Keep a log of your prompts and their outcomes. This can be a personal resource for understanding which types of prompts work best in various situations.

Because conversational AI is evolving so rapidly, that means the art of prompt engineering is constantly evolving along with it. But the core principle remains: communicate effectively with the AI. By staying informed and practicing diligently, you can harness the full potential of ChatGPT to accomplish a wide range of tasks with greater efficiency and creativity.

Chapter Wrap-Up

That concludes our excursion through the art of prompt engineering, and now you have the essential skills to create effective prompts that utilize the full potential of ChatGPT. This chapter has guided you through the nuances of balancing information, tailoring your prompts to achieve clarity, and strategically guiding the AI to generate the most relevant and useful responses. You've learned how to fine-tune your inquiries to communicate effectively with this sophisticated tool, a skill that will undoubtedly enhance your interactions and outcomes with AI.

In the following chapters, we will shift our focus from crafting prompts to applying these skills in various scenarios. We will explore the real-world applications of ChatGPT and demonstrate how it can be a powerful ally in different domains, whether it's for personal development, professional tasks, creative projects, complex problem-solving, or starting a business. You'll witness the versatility of ChatGPT, exploring its capacity to transform industries, streamline workflows, and even inspire innovation.

The upcoming chapter promises to broaden your perspective, showcasing the practicality and transformative potential of ChatGPT when applied to everyday challenges and opportunities. So, let's step forward, ready to apply our refined skills in prompt engineering to real-world situations, unlocking new possibilities and discovering the expansive utility of ChatGPT in our lives and society.

Share Your Thoughts, Make an Impact

Hi there! Quick question: Would you help a fellow learner by taking 60 seconds to leave a review of this book?

Your insights could guide someone eager to learn about ChatGPT. Just a few words from you might make a big difference for someone else looking to boost their productivity, income, and creativity with AI.

Your feedback is invaluable in helping others discover how they can benefit from this book.

Scan the QR code to leave your review. It only takes 60 seconds!

Thank you for contributing to our learning community. Your support is greatly appreciated!

ModernMind Publications

Chapter 5

Transforming Industries through Real-World Applications

In this chapter, we explore the practical applications of ChatGPT, highlighting its significant impact across various industries. As an advanced artificial intelligence model, ChatGPT has moved beyond theoretical use cases to become a crucial tool in many sectors. From human resources and customer service to education and more, its ability to produce human-like text has transformed how tasks are performed and managed. Through a collection of real-world examples and case studies, we will examine how ChatGPT serves not only as a technological breakthrough but also as a driver of operational efficiency, enhanced service delivery, and greater engagement. This exploration will showcase the model's adaptability, emphasizing its role in streamlining processes, offering support, and sparking innovations that tackle complex issues and cater to a wide range of needs.

ChatGPT in Content Creation

In the digital age, content is king. The demand for high-quality, engaging content across various platforms is at an all-time high. However, the process of content creation can be time-consuming and challenging, especially for individuals and businesses with limited resources. This is where ChatGPT steps in as a game-changer. Let's explore how ChatGPT can revolutionize content creation, making it more efficient and creative.

Streamlining Blog Post Creation

Imagine Alex, who runs a thriving coffee shop and aims to share his passion for coffee through a weekly blog. Balancing the demands of his business with content creation can be daunting. Enter ChatGPT: Alex outlines his ideas for posts, such as "The Art of Coffee Tasting" or "Sustainable Coffee Sourcing," and ChatGPT quickly provides him with well-thought-out drafts. These drafts serve as a robust starting point, significantly cutting down the time Alex spends writing, allowing him to infuse his personal experiences and expertise before sharing them with his audience.

Utilizing ChatGPT for content creation, Alex not only maintains a consistent blogging schedule but also sees a notable increase in online engagement and foot traffic to his coffee shop. This success story underscores the impact of leveraging AI for content generation.

Enhancing Freelance Writing with AI

Freelance writers, constantly juggling multiple projects and deadlines, can find ChatGPT to be an invaluable asset. By using ChatGPT to brainstorm ideas or create detailed outlines for articles, they can streamline their writing process. This not only saves time but also enhances the quality of their work, allowing them to take on more projects and increase their earnings.

Exercise: Generating an Article Outline

- **Objective**: Use ChatGPT to create an outline for an article titled "The Future of Remote Work."

Steps:

1. Provide ChatGPT with the article title and ask for key points to cover, such as technological advancements, workspace trends, and the impact on work life balance.
2. Refine the generated outline by asking for subpoints under each key area.
3. Use the final outline as a guide to write a comprehensive and engaging article.

Revolutionizing Educational Content with ChatGPT

Educators, too, can leverage ChatGPT for curriculum planning and creating educational materials. By inputting the syllabus or learning objectives, ChatGPT can suggest lesson plans, activities, and even draft educational content that is tailored to students' needs, making the curriculum more engaging and effective.

Innovating Video Script Dialogues

Consider Arjun, an aspiring documentary filmmaker focusing on environmental conservation. He employs ChatGPT to draft dialogues and narrative scripts, feeding it information about his topics and the messages he wants to convey. ChatGPT assists in developing compelling narratives that engage viewers, enabling Arjun to dedicate more time to research, filming, and editing.

With ChatGPT's assistance, Arjun completes his documentary in record time, with the final product praised for its engaging narrative and impactful message. This highlights the efficiency and creativity AI can bring to content creation within the film industry.

ChatGPT's ability to assist with content creation across various fields and formats is transforming the topography of digital content. From blogging and freelance writing to education and filmmaking, the use of AI not only saves time but also enhances creativity and productivity. As we continue to explore and expand the capabilities of AI tools like ChatGPT, the possibilities for content creation are boundless, opening new doors for creators and businesses alike.

Expediting Customer Support with ChatGPT

Dealing with customer inquiries is a crucial yet often monotonous and resource-intensive aspect of business operations. The advent of advanced AI tools like ChatGPT presents an opportunity to optimize customer support services.

Automating Routine Inquiries

Consider the scenario of a burgeoning tech startup that deploys ChatGPT to tackle the influx of routine customer inquiries. This integration allows the startup's customer support team to channel their energies toward addressing more nuanced and complex customer issues. With ChatGPT autonomously managing the common questions about product usage, troubleshooting, or account management, the support staff's burden is significantly lightened.

Enhancing Response Times

The infusion of ChatGPT into customer service systems is a strategic move for businesses aiming to deliver prompt replies to customer queries. A retail company, for example, could implement a ChatGPT-driven chatbot on its website and customer service channels. This bot would be capable of immediately answering frequently asked questions regarding product features, stock levels, delivery timescales, and return policies. Such a solution not only boosts customer satisfaction by providing instant support but also allows human customer service agents to devote more time to intricate customer concerns that require a personal touch and in-depth problem-solving.

The dual benefits of automating routine support tasks and improving response efficiency make ChatGPT an invaluable asset in the domain of customer support.

ChatGPT in Education and Learning

ChatGPT is reshaping education and learning, offering a plethora of innovative applications that cater to diverse learning styles and individual needs while fostering interactive engagement and personalized experiences.

Personalized Learning Experiences

One of the most compelling aspects of ChatGPT in education is its ability to provide tailored learning experiences. Take, for instance, a language learning application that harnesses ChatGPT's capabilities to create customized exercises based on each user's proficiency level. Through sophisticated analysis of user interactions and responses, ChatGPT can dynamically adjust the difficulty, pacing, and content of exercises, ensuring an optimized learning trajectory for learners at every stage of their language acquisition voyage.

Not only does this personalized approach boost learner motivation and retention, but it also addresses the diverse needs and learning preferences of individual students. For example, a student struggling with grammar concepts may receive targeted exercises and explanations tailored to their specific areas of weakness, while a more advanced learner may be challenged with complex vocabulary and conversational scenarios to further refine their language skills.

Curriculum Development and Support

In addition to facilitating personalized learning experiences, ChatGPT is increasingly being employed by educators to streamline curriculum development and provide supplemental support to students. By leveraging ChatGPT's natural language processing capabilities, teachers can generate a wide range of educational materials, from quiz questions and interactive lessons to explanatory texts and learning aids.

Furthermore, ChatGPT serves as a valuable resource for educators seeking to enhance their instructional strategies and adapt their teaching approaches to meet the diverse needs of students. For instance, teachers can utilize ChatGPT to generate alternative explanations or examples for complex concepts, catering to different learning preferences and cognitive styles within the classroom. Additionally, ChatGPT can assist educators in designing differentiated instruction plans that accommodate students with varying levels of prior knowledge and skill mastery, ensuring that all learners have access to meaningful learning opportunities.

Interactive Learning Platforms

Online tutoring platforms and educational websites are harnessing the power of ChatGPT to create immersive and interactive learning experiences for students. By integrating ChatGPT into their platforms, these services enable students to engage in simulated one-on-one conversations, receive personalized feedback, and access on-demand assistance from virtual tutors.

For example, imagine an online tutoring platform where students can interact with a ChatGPT-powered virtual tutor in real time, asking questions, receiving explanations, and practicing skills through interactive dialogue. This interactive learning environment not only fosters deeper engagement and comprehension but also provides students with immediate feedback and support, facilitating their academic growth and development.

In summary, ChatGPT represents a paradigm shift in education, offering unprecedented opportunities for personalized learning, curriculum development, and interactive engagement. As educators continue to explore and harness the potential of ChatGPT in the classroom, the possibilities for transforming teaching and learning experiences are limitless, paving the way for a more inclusive, adaptive, and effective educational ecosystem.

If you're interested in diving much deeper into this topic, feel free to check out my other book, "Teaching With AI: Empowering Educators For the Future Classroom - Unlock Learning Potential, Save Time, and Simplify the Complexities of Integration in Education."

Leveraging ChatGPT for Business Intelligence

ChatGPT is not only a powerful tool for facilitating human-like conversations but also a valuable asset in the realm of business intelligence, enabling organizations to extract actionable insights from vast volumes of data and make informed decisions.

Generating Insights from Data

One of the key applications of ChatGPT in business intelligence is its ability to analyze data and extract meaningful insights. For example, consider a marketing agency that utilizes ChatGPT to sift through customer feedback from various sources such as surveys, social media, and reviews. By processing this unstructured data, ChatGPT can identify emerging trends, customer preferences, and pain points, providing the agency with valuable insights that inform the development of more targeted and effective marketing strategies.

Similarly, businesses can leverage ChatGPT to monitor social media sentiment surrounding their products or services in real time. By analyzing user-generated content across different platforms, ChatGPT can gauge public perception, identify potential issues or opportunities, and help organizations proactively respond to customer feedback, thereby enhancing brand reputation and customer satisfaction.

Competitive Edge through Informed Decision Making

Implementing ChatGPT in business intelligence can confer a competitive edge by enabling organizations to make data-driven decisions with greater speed and accuracy. Take, for instance, a financial services firm like PQR that leverages ChatGPT to analyze market trends, news articles, and financial reports. By processing vast amounts of textual data,

ChatGPT can identify patterns, correlations, and emerging opportunities in the market, empowering PQR to make timely and informed investment decisions.

Furthermore, ChatGPT's ability to generate human-like responses and engage in natural language interactions can enhance the efficiency of business intelligence processes. For instance, employees can query ChatGPT to retrieve relevant information from internal databases, conduct conversational analysis of market research reports, or even automate routine tasks such as report generation or data summarization.

ChatGPT offers businesses a versatile and scalable solution for extracting insights from data, enabling them to gain a deeper understanding of customer behavior, market dynamics, and competitive landscape. By harnessing the power of ChatGPT in business intelligence, organizations can drive innovation, mitigate risks, and gain a competitive edge in today's rapidly evolving business environment.

Legal Assistance with ChatGPT

ChatGPT has emerged as a transformative force within the legal industry, furnishing lawyers with an array of invaluable tools to augment their practice. Consider Olivia, a seasoned attorney grappling with the relentless demands of legal research and document preparation. Amidst a heavy caseload that demanded her full attention, Olivia explored the potential of integrating ChatGPT into her workflow.

Traditionally, delving into case law and statutes with meticulous detail posed significant challenges for legal study. However, Olivia swiftly recognized the time-saving capabilities of ChatGPT and began to rely on its assistance. For instance, when tasked with unraveling complex legal precedents, Olivia found that ChatGPT provided concise and accurate summaries tailored to her specific inquiries, expediting her comprehension of crucial information. This newfound efficiency revolutionized Olivia's ability to navigate the competitive terrain of the legal profession, empowering her to construct more compelling legal arguments and stay ahead of the curve

Moreover, ChatGPT revolutionized the process of drafting everyday legal documents for Olivia. By inputting the requirements for various legal documents, such as contracts and agreements, Olivia entrusted ChatGPT to generate initial drafts. For example, Olivia could simply provide ChatGPT with the key terms and conditions of a contract, and the tool would swiftly produce a comprehensive draft. This streamlined approach not only expedited the document preparation process but also ensured accuracy and consistency across multiple iterations, thereby enhancing Olivia's productivity and enabling her to devote more time to strategic legal analysis.

In client meetings and courtroom proceedings, Olivia leveraged ChatGPT to access real-time information swiftly. For instance, during a deposition, Olivia could input specific legal queries into ChatGPT, enabling her to retrieve relevant case law and statutes on the spot. This real-time assistance proved invaluable in navigating complex legal scenarios with agility and confidence, enabling Olivia to make well-informed decisions promptly, even under pressure.

In summary, ChatGPT has become an indispensable asset in Olivia's legal toolkit, empowering her to navigate the intricacies of legal practice with efficiency and confidence. Whether unraveling complex legal precedents, drafting detailed legal documents, or accessing real-time information during client meetings and courtroom proceedings, ChatGPT has proven to be a game-changer in optimizing legal workflows and enhancing overall productivity.

Human Resources Assistance

ChatGPT is a powerful asset for HR professionals, offering innovative solutions to streamline and standardize HR tasks. One significant application is in writing job descriptions. By leveraging ChatGPT, HR managers can quickly create detailed and engaging initial drafts for job listings based on specific requirements, streamlining the recruitment process. This automation allows HR teams to focus on more strategic aspects of hiring.

For instance, Mark, an HR specialist, utilized ChatGPT to efficiently produce job descriptions for various openings within his company. By inputting key skills and responsibilities, he obtained comprehensive, tailored job descriptions, significantly speeding up the process.

Furthermore, ChatGPT can assist in handling frequent employee inquiries about company policies, benefits, and procedures. Implementing ChatGPT to address these common questions can free up HR staff to focus on more complex tasks by providing quick and accurate responses, enhancing overall efficiency.

ChatGPT also plays a crucial role early in the hiring process by helping to filter candidates. It can introduce potential employees to the company culture and benefits, improving their engagement and perception of the company. This use of ChatGPT not only enhances the candidate experience but also positions the company as a desirable employer.

In conclusion, ChatGPT's application in real-world scenarios underscores its transformative potential across various industries and professions. From streamlining HR processes, enhancing customer service, to supporting educational initiatives, ChatGPT has demonstrated its versatility and efficiency. By automating routine tasks, providing personalized interactions, and offering scalable solutions, it allows organizations to focus on strategic growth and innovation. As we've explored through diverse case studies, ChatGPT's ability to understand and generate human-like text opens up new avenues for improving operational efficiencies, enhancing user experiences, and creating more engaging and interactive platforms. As technology continues to evolve, the potential for ChatGPT to drive further innovation and reshape industries is immense. Embracing these advancements will be key to harnessing the full power of AI in solving real-world challenges and unlocking new opportunities for progress and excellence

Chapter 6
Boost Your Productivity

In today's dynamic and fast-paced world, efficiency is crucial to stay ahead. Fortunately, with ChatGPT, increasing your productivity has become more accessible than ever before. This chapter will explore practical strategies for utilizing ChatGPT to revolutionize your workflow and achieve more in less time. Throughout this chapter, we'll discuss a range of techniques for leveraging ChatGPT's capabilities. From automating repetitive tasks to optimizing time management, enhancing communication and collaboration, offering personalized assistance, and supporting learning and skill development, there's a wealth of possibilities for everyone. Whether you're a professional seeking to streamline your workload, a student aiming to excel academically, or an individual striving to make the most of your time, this chapter has something for you.

Automating Routine Tasks

Task automation has become a cornerstone of productivity in modern workplaces. It's also not a new concept in the home if you have a dishwasher or washing machine. By delegating repetitive tasks to technology, individuals can save time and focus their energy on more strategic endeavors. In this section, we'll explore the concept of task automation and how ChatGPT can be a valuable tool in streamlining routine responsibilities.

How ChatGPT Streamlines Repetitive Tasks

ChatGPT offers a versatile solution for automating various routine tasks, including email drafting, scheduling, and data entry. Whether it's composing personalized emails, setting up appointments, or entering data into spreadsheets, ChatGPT can handle these tasks efficiently and effectively.

Case Study: Malaika's Experience with ChatGPT

Malaika, a marketing expert with a busy schedule, found herself spending a significant amount of time on administrative tasks such as drafting client emails and managing appointments. Frustrated by the time-consuming nature of these tasks, she decided to explore the potential of ChatGPT. By integrating ChatGPT into her workflow, Malaika was able to automate the process of composing client emails and scheduling appointments. This not only saved her valuable time but also ensured consistency and accuracy in her communications.

Exercise:

1. Take a moment to identify three repetitive tasks in your daily routine or work responsibilities. Consider tasks such as responding to emails, scheduling meetings, creating a meal plan, or entering data into spreadsheets.
2. Once you've identified these tasks, think about how ChatGPT could automate or simplify them for you.

By leveraging ChatGPT's capabilities for task automation, individuals like Malaika can reclaim valuable time and focus on activities that drive productivity and innovation. As we continue exploring the possibilities of ChatGPT, remember to consider how automation can streamline your workflow and enhance your overall efficiency.

Improving Time Management

Effective time management is essential for maximizing productivity and achieving goals efficiently. In this section, we'll explore the importance of managing time effectively and how ChatGPT can serve as a valuable tool in this endeavor.

The Importance of Effective Time Management

Time is a finite resource, and how we allocate it directly impacts our productivity and success. By effectively managing our time, we can prioritize tasks, minimize procrastination, and ensure that important deadlines are met. Effective time management allows individuals to maintain focus, minimize distractions, and make the most of each day.

How ChatGPT Assists with Time Management

ChatGPT offers a range of features to assist with time management, including scheduling, reminders, and time tracking. Users can input tasks, set reminders, and organize their schedules in a conversational manner. Whether it's scheduling meetings, setting deadlines, or tracking time spent on specific activities, ChatGPT can help individuals stay organized and on track.

Here are a few simple example prompts that someone could use to leverage ChatGPT for time management tasks:

- **Scheduling Meetings:** *"Can you help me create a schedule for my team meetings next week, considering we need to meet twice, avoiding Wednesday and Friday afternoons?"*
- **Setting Deadlines:** *"I need to outline project milestones for the next quarter. Could you assist me in setting deadlines, starting from next week, for a project that should be completed over three months?"*

- **Tracking Time:**"*How can I track the time I spend on my writing project daily, ensuring I dedicate at least two hours each afternoon?*"

Case Study: Smith's Experience with ChatGPT

Smith, a project manager, found himself struggling to keep track of deadlines and stay organized amidst his busy schedule. He decided to incorporate ChatGPT into his workflow to help manage his projects more effectively. By using ChatGPT to set up automatic reminders for project milestones, track progress, and allocate time for long-term planning, Smith was able to streamline his workflow and ensure that projects were completed on time and within budget.

Exercise

Let's take a moment to put ChatGPT to work for our own time management needs.

1. Using ChatGPT, create a sample weekly schedule that includes your tasks, appointments, and deadlines. Experiment with different ways to prioritize tasks and allocate time for both work and personal activities.
2. Once you've created your schedule, reflect on how this approach could improve your time management skills and enhance your overall productivity.

By leveraging ChatGPT's features for time management, individuals like Smith can effectively prioritize tasks, stay organized, and make the most of their time. As we continue exploring the capabilities of ChatGPT, remember to consider how its time management features can help you optimize your workflow and achieve your goals more efficiently.

Enhancing Communication and Collaboration

Effective communication and collaboration are essential for the success of any team, especially in diverse and multicultural environments. In this section, we'll delve into how ChatGPT serves as a powerful tool for fostering communication and collaboration within teams, transcending language barriers, and enabling seamless collaboration.

Exploring ChatGPT's Facilitation of Communication

ChatGPT revolutionizes team communication by offering a platform for seamless interaction, irrespective of language differences. Its advanced natural language processing capabilities enable it to understand and respond to messages in multiple languages, promoting inclusivity and ensuring that every team member can actively participate in discussions and contribute their insights.

For example, imagine a global team working on a project, with members from different countries speaking various languages. ChatGPT can facilitate smooth communication by instantly translating messages between team members, allowing everyone to understand and engage with the discussion effectively. This ensures that language differences do not hinder collaboration and that diverse perspectives can be leveraged to drive the project forward.

Beyond its role as a language translator, ChatGPT excels in various communication-related tasks. It can summarize lengthy documents or discussions, distilling key points and enabling team members to grasp complex information quickly. For instance, during a team meeting where multiple ideas are being discussed, ChatGPT can provide a concise summary of the discussion, ensuring that everyone is on the same page and facilitating more efficient decision-making.

Additionally, ChatGPT provides real-time feedback, enhancing the quality of discussions and fostering a culture of collaboration and continuous improvement within teams. For example, if a team member presents an idea during a brainstorming session, ChatGPT can offer constructive feedback or suggest alternative approaches, encouraging open dialogue and refinement of ideas.

Case Study: Multicultural Team Collaboration with ChatGPT:

Consider a case study where a multinational company's marketing team utilized ChatGPT to overcome language barriers and streamline document collaboration. Despite members hailing from diverse linguistic backgrounds, ChatGPT's translation and summarization features facilitated smooth communication and enabled effective collaboration on projects. This case study underscores ChatGPT's potential to break down barriers and foster a cohesive team environment.

For instance, imagine a marketing team working on a campaign targeting multiple regions with different languages. ChatGPT can assist in translating marketing materials, ensuring consistency and accuracy across all versions. Additionally, it can summarize feedback from stakeholders, allowing the team to focus on implementing actionable insights and improving the campaign's effectiveness.

Exercise: Blog Article Summarization

Practice summarizing a blog article using ChatGPT with this simple exercise:

1. **Choose an Article:** Pick a blog post with substantial content.
2. **Read Carefully:** Understand the main ideas and key arguments.
3. **Identify Key Points:** Highlight central themes and important details.
4. **Summarize with ChatGPT:** Input the article into ChatGPT and request a summary.
5. **Review & Reflect:** Evaluate the summary's accuracy and completeness.
6. **Bonus:** Translate the summary into another language.

By summarizing articles with ChatGPT, you'll enhance your comprehension skills and gain valuable insights into effective summarization techniques.

Providing Personalized Assistance

ChatGPT goes beyond basic tasks like summarization and translation, excelling in delivering personalized assistance that aligns closely with your unique preferences and requirements. This section will discuss how ChatGPT's tailored solutions and recommendations can significantly enhance your productivity.

ChatGPT's Personalization Abilities

ChatGPT is distinguished by its ability to understand and adapt to your individual needs, offering recommendations that range from relevant resources to productivity-enhancing tools, all personalized to fit your specific situation. Its assistance is designed to connect with you on a personal level, thereby enhancing your overall productivity.

Leveraging its advanced algorithms and vast knowledge base, ChatGPT provides solutions that are custom-fit to your preferences, goals, and working style. It intelligently processes your queries, history, and context to offer advice that's not just relevant but also actionable, covering everything from task management strategies to optimizing your daily workflow, ensuring that the guidance you receive is perfectly suited to your needs and aspirations.

Case Study: ChatGPT's Personalized Recommendations:

Imagine a scenario where an individual seeks assistance in improving their time management skills. Through an interactive conversation with ChatGPT, the user shares details about their productivity goals, work habits, and challenges they face. Leveraging this information, ChatGPT generates personalized recommendations tailored to the user's specific needs. These recommendations may include time management strategies, productivity hacks, and relevant resources curated to address the user's unique circumstances. As a result, the user gains valuable insights and actionable advice to enhance their productivity and achieve their goals more effectively.

Exercise: Evaluating Personalized Recommendations

1. **Talk to ChatGPT:** Initiate a conversation with ChatGPT, outlining your productivity goals, preferred working methods, and any challenges you face. Ask ChatGPT how you can reach your productivity goals and address the challenges.
2. **Review Recommendations:** Evaluate the recommendations provided by ChatGPT, considering their relevance, feasibility, and potential effectiveness in addressing your productivity goals and challenges.
3. **Identify Actionable Insights:** Identify actionable insights and key takeaways from ChatGPT's recommendations that you find most compelling and suitable for implementation.
4. **Plan Implementation:** Develop a plan for integrating the recommended strategies into your productivity workflows, considering how they align with your goals and working style. (HINT: You can use ChatGPT to help you with this, too.)

By harnessing ChatGPT's prowess in providing personalized assistance, users can access tailored solutions and recommendations that empower them to excel in their productivity endeavors. Through interactive engagement, evaluation, and refinement, users can fine-tune their productivity workflows and unlock new levels of efficiency and effectiveness in their daily lives.

Supporting Learning and Skill Development

ChatGPT extends its utility beyond conventional tasks, becoming an invaluable aid in facilitating learning and skill development. Let's explore how ChatGPT fosters educational growth and provides tailored assistance across diverse learning domains.

Exploring ChatGPT's Educational Role

ChatGPT serves as a versatile learning companion, offering support in various educational endeavors. Whether learners seek clarification on complex topics, require assistance with problem-solving, or desire to explore new concepts, ChatGPT stands ready to provide personalized guidance and explanations.

From mathematical problem-solving to scientific concepts and historical events, ChatGPT serves as a reliable source of information, helping learners deepen their understanding and master challenging topics.

Skill Development and Practice

Beyond traditional educational assistance, ChatGPT offers opportunities for skill development and practice. Whether learners aim to improve their writing skills, enhance their creativity, or refine their critical thinking abilities, ChatGPT provides interactive exercises and prompts to stimulate growth and development in these areas.

Case Study: Professional Development with ChatGPT

Imagine a scenario where professionals seek to enhance their project management skills with ChatGPT's assistance. By engaging with ChatGPT, professionals can receive personalized guidance and advice on project planning, execution strategies, and problem-solving approaches. ChatGPT offers tailored recommendations and insights based on the specific challenges and objectives of each professional, empowering them to excel in their roles and advance their careers.

Exercise: Enhancing Your Critical Thinking

This exercise will sharpen your critical thinking skills by encouraging you to scrutinize responses, formulate counterarguments, and apply analytical reasoning, thereby enhancing your ability to engage with complex ideas thoughtfully and critically.

- **Pick a Subject**: Start by choosing a subject you're interested in or curious about.
- **Craft a Question**: Create a challenging question related to your chosen subject.
- **Consult ChatGPT**: Pose your question to ChatGPT and see what it comes up with.
- **Review the Answers**: Take a close look at what ChatGPT has replied and think about the reasoning behind each response.
- **Challenge the Answers**: Try to come up with arguments or reasons that might question or contradict ChatGPT's responses.
- **Reflect on the Experience**: Think about how this activity made you question or consider new perspectives.
- **Use What You've Learned**: Think about how you can apply this enhanced critical thinking approach to situations or problems in your daily life.

Exercise: Exploring Any Topic with ChatGPT

This exercise will teach you how to broaden your knowledge on a chosen subject by engaging with ChatGPT's insights, fostering a deeper understanding of the topic, and enabling you to apply this enhanced comprehension to real-world contexts.

1. **Select a Topic:** Choose a subject you want to learn about.
2. **Ask Questions:** Pose questions to ChatGPT about the topic.
3. **Engage:** ChatGPT will provide insights and explanations.
4. **Reflect and Apply:** Use the information gained to deepen your understanding and apply it to real-world situations.

By leveraging ChatGPT's educational assistance and skill development capabilities, learners and professionals alike can easily pursue continuous growth and improvement. Through interactive engagement and targeted practice, individuals can acquire new knowledge, refine their skills, and achieve their learning goals with ChatGPT as their trusted guide.

Chapter Wrap-Up

In wrapping up, we've immersed ourselves in the diverse ways ChatGPT can revolutionize productivity across different spheres of life and work. From simplifying mundane tasks to facilitating communication, aiding learning, and offering tailored assistance, ChatGPT presents numerous avenues for improvement and advancement.

Throughout this chapter, we've observed how ChatGPT streamlines operations, furnishes valuable insights and empowers users to attain their objectives more effectively. By leveraging ChatGPT's functionalities, you can reach heightened levels of productivity, innovation, and efficiency in your pursuits.

As you utilize ChatGPT in your daily routines, remember to explore its capabilities and experiment with its features. Whether you're automating tasks, seeking educational aid, or honing your critical thinking skills, ChatGPT is there to support you in your quest for productivity.

Embrace ChatGPT's transformative potential and seamlessly integrate it into your workflows. By doing so, you'll not only streamline your tasks and accomplish them more proficiently but also open up avenues for further growth and success.

Chapter 7
Creating Monetizable Content and Products

Harnessing the power of ChatGPT can open up a myriad of opportunities for creating value and earning income. Chapter 7 embarks on a pragmatic exploration of practical approaches for entrepreneurs and creators to transform ChatGPT's capabilities into profitable ventures. From conceptualizing AI-driven products to disseminating knowledge via digital books and courses, this chapter provides a blueprint for individuals aiming to monetize their innovations with ChatGPT.

We'll dissect the strategies behind crafting ChatGPT-powered applications that answer real-world needs, such as customer support and productivity enhancement. Then, we'll navigate the realm of digital publishing, offering guidance on creating compelling e-books and courses that cater to the growing demand for AI education. Finally, we'll look at how to leverage online platforms like blogs and YouTube channels, turning a passion for AI into a source of income through engaging content and innovative marketing techniques.

In this chapter, we're not just covering the 'how-to'; we're equipping you with the insights to build a sustainable and scalable digital business model centered around ChatGPT's transformative technology.

Setting Expectations: The Truth About Monetizing ChatGPT

Before we begin these following two chapters on using ChatGPT to earn an income, it's essential to confront some common misconceptions head-on. My own experience over the last half-year has been enlightening: making money with ChatGPT and other AI tools requires real work and a willingness to learn continually. Let's debunk some common myths about making money with ChatGPT and AI:

The Myth of Overnight Success: I know, we've all heard those dazzling stories of folks who seemingly struck gold on their first try. But let's be real—most success stories are like icebergs, with the bulk of hard work hidden beneath the surface. Using ChatGPT to make money isn't a magic spell. It demands your time, creativity, and a bit of elbow grease to really shine.

The 'No Skills Needed' Fallacy: There's this notion that AI is your golden ticket to the land where no learning or expertise is required. However, in our world, ChatGPT is a sidekick, not the superhero. It amplifies your talents and knowledge, so honing your writing, marketing, or tech skills will only strengthen your outputs with ChatGPT.

The Automation Dream: Some of us dream of a set-it-and-forget-it income stream where AI does all the heavy lifting. But here's the scoop—ChatGPT is more of a co-pilot than an autopilot. It thrives under your guidance and oversight, ensuring that the end product aligns perfectly with your vision.

Replacing Jobs? Not Quite: In the swirl of excitement, it's easy to think that ChatGPT could replace entire jobs, giving you a shortcut to earnings. In truth, it's about collaboration. ChatGPT enhances your work, helping you to be more productive and creative, but it doesn't eliminate the need for your unique human touch.

Guaranteed Profits? If Only: I wish I could say that every venture with ChatGPT turns to gold, but business is still business. Profitability is a dance with many steps, including market demand, execution, and innovation. There's no one-size-fits-all guarantee.

Unique Content Creation? Not So Fast: Sure, ChatGPT can churn out content, but it's not a secret backdoor to top Google rankings. Quality content requires a human editor's touch, and with search engines getting wise to AI, authenticity and originality have never been more important.

Unlimited Scalability? Check Your Resources: Scaling any business has its challenges, and although ChatGPT is incredibly scalable, it's not free from the laws of economics. Resources, both computational and human, will always be a factor.

Ease of Monetization? It's Complicated: Finally, while there are straightforward ways to monetize content, like ads or subscriptions, each strategy requires a tailored approach. You'll need to really understand your audience and stay agile to keep up with the market as it continues to change.

There's no magic formula—what works for one person might not work for another, and AI is always changing. Getting my knowledge and skill to where it is today has been as much about understanding these nuances as it has been about celebrating the victories along the way.

So, consider this not just as advice but as a field report from the trenches of AI monetization. Making money with ChatGPT can be a part of your income stream if you approach it with the right mindset: one that values consistent innovation and strategic planning. The opportunities are real, but they demand your effort, engagement, and creativity.

For those willing to put in the work, the possibilities are truly limitless.

Share Your Expertise with Online Courses

The creation and sale of online courses have opened a new frontier for experts and educators alike. This section will navigate you through transforming your knowledge into a profitable online course. With advancements in AI and accessible platforms, we'll give an overview of what it takes to craft a compelling curriculum, produce engaging content, and reach learners around the globe.

Identifying a Course Topic: The first step in creating an online course is much like that of writing an e-book: finding the right topic. It should be an area where you hold expertise or a unique perspective. Utilize ChatGPT to explore what potential students are curious about and what gaps exist in the current online course offerings. ChatGPT can help brainstorm ideas, suggest course outlines, and even help you refine your course objectives to ensure they resonate with your target audience.

Curriculum Development: With your topic in hand, it's time to flesh out your curriculum. Break down your course into digestible modules and lessons. Here, ChatGPT can assist by generating content ideas, creating lesson outlines, or even writing lesson summaries. Use the AI to help explain complex concepts in simple terms or to generate quizzes and interactive content that can make your course more engaging.

Creating Course Material: Creating compelling course materials is key. You might include videos, written content, and interactive sessions. ChatGPT can be instrumental here too; for example, use it to generate scripts for your video lessons or to create written guides and resources. Tools like Loom can help you record and edit video content, while Canva can be used to design appealing graphics and presentation slides. If you want to take it a step further, there are AI tools out there that can help you create videos with avatars included. Synthesia is an example, just be careful you don't choose to compromise the quality of your product in doing so.

Platform Selection and Course Setup: Choosing the right platform is crucial for your course's success. Platforms like Udemy and Coursera are popular, but there are also others like Teachable and Skillshare. Each platform has its own set of tools and audience. Once selected, use ChatGPT to craft a compelling course description and to determine the best SEO practices to improve the course's visibility on the platform.

Marketing Your Online Course: Marketing is vital to attract students. Use AI to analyze the market and create targeted advertising campaigns. ChatGPT can help write ad copy, create promotional emails, and generate content for social media to drum up interest. Consider using targeted Facebook ads or LinkedIn messages, and use AI to test different marketing messages and strategies to see what resonates with your potential students.

Case Study: 'Mastering Digital Photography'

Let's take the example of Sheryl, a professional photographer who created an online course teaching digital photography basics. Sheryl used ChatGPT to define a curriculum that covered gaps she noticed in other photography courses. She used AI to help script her video lessons, which she then recorded using user-friendly video tools. For marketing, she utilized AI to identify the most effective channels to reach aspiring photographers and to create captivating promotional materials. As a result, Sheryl's course quickly gained popularity and became a top-rated course on the platform she chose.

Starting a ChatGPT Blog or YouTube Channel

In a digital ecosystem brimming with content creators, standing out with a ChatGPT blog or YouTube channel can be your gateway to connecting with a tech-savvy audience and monetizing your insights into the world of AI and machine learning.

Defining Your Niche and Content Strategy: The AI landscape is expansive, so carving out your niche is essential. Whether your strength lies in explaining the intricacies of machine learning models or in demonstrating practical applications of ChatGPT, your content should cater to specific interests. A content strategy that aligns with your expertise will not only attract the right audience but also establish you as an authority in the field. Plan your blog posts or videos around key themes, such as troubleshooting common ChatGPT issues, sharing innovative uses, or offering tutorials for developers.

Establishing Your Platform: With a clear direction, the next step is to build your platform. For bloggers, WordPress or Wix offers customizable templates and plugins to get started. As a YouTuber, creating a channel with a catchy name and professional-looking graphics is key. Your platform should reflect a cohesive brand image that resonates with your content strategy.

Content Creation: The value you provide through your content is what will retain your audience. High-quality, engaging, and informative content that solves problems or answers questions will build your reputation. Use ChatGPT to brainstorm content ideas or even draft initial outlines for your pieces. Diversify your content with interviews, reviews, and case studies to keep your audience engaged.

Leveraging ChatGPT and Other AI Tools: ChatGPT can be a powerful ally in content creation. Use it to automate initial drafts or generate creative ideas. Incorporate SEO tools powered by AI to optimize your content for search engines and analytics tools to gain insights into your audience's behavior and preferences.

Building an Audience: Growth is about visibility and engagement. Implement SEO best practices to ensure your blog or videos rank high in search results. Google and YouTube have very different algorithms, so be sure to do your research on how to get your content to rank. Engage with your community by responding to comments, hosting Q&A sessions, and being active on social media platforms. Growing your audience also means staying updated with AI trends to keep your content relevant.

Monetization: As your audience grows, so do your monetization opportunities. Apply for Google AdSense to start earning revenue from ads on your blog. For YouTube, once you meet the eligibility criteria, you can join the YouTube Partner Program. Collaborate with AI-centric businesses for sponsored content, and use affiliate marketing to recommend products you trust, earning a commission in the process.

Scaling Your Platform. Monitor your blog's or channel's analytics to understand what resonates with your audience. Scale your content by investing in marketing or collaborating with other content creators. Always be on the lookout for opportunities to expand your reach, like guest blogging or cross-platform promotions.

Case Studies

Consider a YouTube channel started by an AI enthusiast, Jake, who shared weekly tutorials on ChatGPT. Over time, he grew his subscriber base significantly, leading to partnerships with AI companies for sponsored videos. Similarly, a blog started by Lisa, a data scientist, gained popularity by offering in-depth analyses of AI trends, leading to a profitable venture through ad revenue and affiliate marketing.

By systematically building and nurturing your ChatGPT-focused platform, you can translate your knowledge and passion into a successful content-driven business. Whether through helpful tutorials, insightful analyses, or innovative applications, your content can enlighten and inspire, all while generating a sustainable income.

Harnessing AI to Write and Sell Books

The fusion of artificial intelligence with our creative endeavors has opened doors to possibilities that once seemed like science fiction. Imagine you're sitting at your desk, pondering over the expanse of knowledge and stories within you, just waiting to be shared with the world. You're not alone in this venture; AI, specifically ChatGPT, is your silent, yet incredibly resourceful partner.

Let's walk through the process of writing and publishing a book – one that's been constructed with the threads of AI's capabilities.

Selecting Your Topic: Choosing the right topic is the foundation of your book. It should be something you're passionate about and knowledgeable in, yet also in demand. Use ChatGPT to tap into current trends and demands. Ask it about popular topics within your area of expertise or interest. Once you have a topic, ChatGPT can help you outline your book, ensuring you cover all the necessary points that a potential reader might expect.

Writing Your Book: The writing process is where you bring your knowledge to life. ChatGPT can assist you by providing information, generating content ideas, or even helping to write sections of your book. Remember, though, that your voice and expertise are irreplaceable—use AI as a tool to enhance your natural writing abilities.

Editing and Formatting: Once your book is written, it's time to edit and format. This step is crucial because a well-edited and formatted book can significantly enhance readability. Use AI tools like Grammarly to catch grammatical mistakes and enhance sentence structure. For formatting, consider AI-powered software that adheres to Amazon Kindle's formatting requirements to ensure your book looks professional and is easy to navigate. Vellum is good example of a formatting software that is easy to learn and us (the downside is it's only available for Mac users).

Publishing on Amazon Kindle: Publishing your book is where your work comes to fruition. With Amazon Kindle Direct Publishing (KDP), you can easily upload your book. ChatGPT can assist in writing a compelling book description and help you determine the best keywords to make your book discoverable. Remember, the Amazon marketplace is massive, and visibility is key to sales.

Marketing Your Book: No book can succeed without proper marketing. AI tools can provide a significant advantage here. Use ChatGPT to create engaging marketing content for your social media, blog posts, or email newsletters. AI can analyze data to pinpoint the best marketing strategies, helping you target your ideal audience effectively.

Developing Chatbots for Customer Support

In customer service, chatbots have revolutionized the way businesses interact with their customers. By integrating the capabilities of ChatGPT, these chatbots can provide nuanced and contextually relevant support, mirroring human interaction with the added benefits of scalability and constant availability. Building a successful chatbot service requires a strategic approach that encompasses market understanding, technical execution, and continuous enhancement.

What it doesn't necessarily demand is that you be steeped in coding or possess extensive technical knowledge. Yes, you do need to be willing to roll up your sleeves to research and learn some other AI tools and software. But today's platforms and tools are designed with user-friendliness in mind, enabling entrepreneurs to harness the power of AI and chatbot technology through intuitive interfaces and no-code solutions. This accessibility opens the door for individuals from diverse backgrounds to create, manage, and deploy chatbots tailored to a variety of customer service needs. With a focus on strategic planning, understanding user needs, and leveraging the right tools, anyone can build a successful chatbot service business, turning innovative ideas into practical solutions without writing a single line of code.

Identify a Niche: The first step is to conduct thorough market research to identify industries with a high volume of customer interactions and a gap in efficient, 24/7 support. For instance, small to medium-sized e-commerce businesses often struggle with providing immediate responses to customer queries. Targeting such a niche where quick, efficient service can lead to higher customer retention rates can be a strategic move.

Understand the Audience: It is crucial to dive deep into the customer psyche of your chosen niche. By analyzing customer service logs, online forums, and feedback surveys, you can compile a comprehensive list of the most frequent customer inquiries and pain points. This data serves as a foundation for developing your chatbot's knowledge base and personality, ensuring it aligns with the expectations and language of your target audience.

Design the Conversation Flow: The conversation flow should be designed to be intuitive, leading the customer through a seamless support experience. Employ user journey mapping techniques to visualize the path a customer would take when interacting with your chatbot. This helps to predict and script effective dialogue for various scenarios, from simple FAQs to complex troubleshooting steps.

Choose Your Platform: Selection of the right platform is essential. If your target businesses mostly interact with customers via their websites, then a web-based chatbot would be appropriate. On the other hand, if their customers are more active on social media, then platforms like Facebook Messenger or WhatsApp might be more suitable.

Build the Chatbot: Leverage platforms like Dialogflow, Microsoft Bot Framework, or Rasa, which provide robust environments to build and deploy chatbots. These platforms offer easy integrations with ChatGPT and other AI services, allowing you to craft a chatbot with sophisticated conversational abilities and the ability to learn from interactions.

Train Your Chatbot: Utilize ChatGPT to train your chatbot with realistic dialogue scenarios tailored to your niche. This training should be an ongoing process, where the chatbot continually learns and improves from each interaction.

Test and Iterate: Extensive testing is non-negotiable. Beta testing with real users can provide invaluable insights into the chatbot's performance and user experience. Collect data, iterate on the design, and refine the conversation flows based on feedback.

Monetization: Develop a business model that provides value to both the end-users and the companies that will utilize your chatbot. A subscription-based model with scalable tiers allows businesses of different sizes to engage with your service. Additionally, you can offer customizations and integrations as part of premium packages.

Case Study: A Success Story

Let's consider a fictional success story that encapsulates the process of building a ChatGPT-powered chatbot business from the ground up.

Background: Selena, an IT consultant with a background in customer support, noticed that small e-commerce fashion brands struggled with providing real-time customer service. Identifying this gap, Selena envisioned a chatbot that could offer instant support for common customer queries, like order tracking and product inquiries.

Development: Selena chose Dialogflow for its advanced AI capabilities and seamless integration with ChatGPT. She designed conversation flows based on common scenarios in the fashion e-commerce space and used ChatGPT to generate realistic dialogue options. She also integrated a sentiment analysis tool to detect when a customer became frustrated, at which point the chatbot would escalate the conversation to a human agent.

Rollout: After a successful pilot with a local fashion brand, where the chatbot reduced response time by 70%, Selena officially launched her business. The chatbot was marketed to e-commerce businesses, emphasizing its 24/7 availability and capability to handle scale during peak shopping seasons.

Monetization and Growth: The company adopted a tiered subscription model, with a free trial period to encourage adoption. The service offered basic chatbot functionalities in its free tier, with advanced features like custom branding and analytics available in premium tiers. As Selena's product proved to increase customer satisfaction and sales, more brands signed up, allowing Selena to reinvest in the business and expand her offerings.

Impact: Selena's business not only provided a valuable service to e-commerce brands but also significantly enhanced the customer shopping experience. By leveraging the power of ChatGPT, Selena turned a market need into a thriving business, demonstrating the potential of AI-powered chatbots in transforming customer service.

By following a similar path, identifying market needs, and systematically developing and refining your product, you too can create a ChatGPT-powered chatbot that not only serves businesses but also contributes to a better customer experience.

Creating Writing Aids and Tools That Enhance Productivity

The demand for high-quality writing aids has surged with the increase in digital content production. Such tools not only assist in creating grammatically sound content but also save time and enhance the overall quality of writing. Establishing a business in this domain involves recognizing a service gap, creating a valuable product, and strategically introducing it to the market. It may also require some technical skill, so if that's not you, you can probably skip this one.

Identify the Gap: Begin with a thorough analysis of existing writing tools. Understand their features, limitations, and user feedback. Identify a niche that is underserved – perhaps a tool that specializes in technical writing, creative storytelling, or academic research papers. Your goal is to pinpoint a specific pain point that your tool can address more effectively than current solutions.

Design the Tool: Design a tool that is comprehensive and user-friendly. Decide whether it will specialize in grammar correction, style improvement, plagiarism detection, or if it will be an all-encompassing solution. Consider how your tool will fit into the user's existing workflow – will it be a web application, a desktop application, or a plug-in for word processors?

Develop the Product: Leverage cutting-edge AI technologies such as OpenAI's GPT-3 or its successors to power your tool. These AI models can provide nuanced understanding and generation of natural language, which is essential for a writing aid. The development phase should focus on creating an intuitive interface that allows users to interact with the AI seamlessly, providing instant suggestions and corrections.

Test Your Product: Testing is a critical step. Assemble a diverse beta tester group that represents your target audience. Collect detailed feedback on the tool's performance in various writing scenarios. Use this data to refine algorithms, fix bugs, and improve the user interface.

Launch and Market: When you launch, ensure your marketing clearly articulates the benefits of your tool – how it saves time, improves writing quality, and integrates smoothly with other tools. Employ content marketing strategies, search engine optimization (SEO), and leverage social media platforms to reach your potential users.

Monetization Strategies: Adopt a monetization model that provides value while generating revenue. A freemium model is often effective, offering basic functionalities for free while charging for advanced features. Alternatively, explore the possibility of a one-time purchase or subscription models. There's also the potential for licensing your tool to educational institutions or businesses.

Case Study

Let's consider a fictional case study of a business that successfully launched a writing aid tool.

Background: Dylan, a software developer and part-time blogger, noticed the lack of a writing aid that catered to both technical writing and creative storytelling. He saw the opportunity for a tool that could assist users in switching between different writing styles seamlessly.

Development: Dylan decided to use the latest AI technology from OpenAI to build his tool. The tool featured grammar and style checkers, a tone adjuster, and a unique storytelling aid for creative writers. He designed it to integrate with popular word processors and online platforms.

Rollout: After developing the tool, Dylan conducted a closed beta test with both technical writers and creative writers. He used their feedback to fine-tune the algorithms, ensuring the suggestions were contextually appropriate and the tool was user-friendly.

Monetization and Growth: Dylan's company was launched with a freemium model, gaining initial traction through content marketing that showcased its unique ability to cater to diverse writing needs. As the user base grew, Alex introduced a premium subscription model with additional features like a plagiarism checker and a more advanced style guide.

Impact: Dylan's creation became a favored tool among professionals and students. Its success was rooted in its dual focus on different writing domains, user-centric design, and leveraging AI to provide real-time, intelligent assistance.

By emulating Dylan's strategic approach to identifying a market need, developing a targeted product, and effectively introducing it to the market, entrepreneurs can create successful writing aid tools. Incorporating additional AI tools and plugins can further refine the product and enhance its capabilities, leading to a sustainable and profitable business.

Chapter Wrap-Up

In this chapter, we have only touched on the potential of earning with ChatGPT. There's a lot more to you to learn here, but digging into the minutiae of each strategy is well beyond the scope of this book. We have discussed how effectively leveraging ChatGPT can open up profitable opportunities in various domains, including business operations, content creation, and customer service. The uphill climb to monetizing ChatGPT requires creativity, strategic thinking, and staying ahead in the rapidly developing AI field.

In the upcoming chapter, we'll go even deeper into the many ways you can monetize your ChatGPT skills to discover new revenue streams. I will share more strategies, inspire innovative thinking, and guide you toward greater success in the world of AI entrepreneurship.

Chapter 8

Monetize Your ChatGPT Expertise

There are other ways that navigating the terrain of artificial intelligence with ChatGPT can transform from a personal passion to a profitable venture. This chapter presents career paths that are more technical in nature than those discussed in the previous chapter. Here, we will discuss turning your curiosity and skill in conversational AI into a profitable consultancy, a vibrant training platform, or a thriving freelance business. We will walk through the steps to identify your unique value proposition, construct a service that speaks to the needs of this AI-driven market, and communicate your expertise in ways that resonate with clients and organizations. It's not just about knowing the tool—it's about crafting a narrative and a business model that makes your knowledge in ChatGPT a sought-after commodity.

Provide Personalized ChatGPT Training for Others

Let's start with a fictional case study. Customized ChatGPT Learning Hub, founded by tech educator Priya, addresses the growing demand for specialized ChatGPT training. Her vision was to craft personalized programs that cater to professionals across various sectors, enhancing their efficiency and skills through AI.

The hub targets key groups like entrepreneurs, writers, and developers, offering a curriculum that evolves from basic ChatGPT understanding to complex applications, combining theoretical knowledge with practical exercises. Utilizing platforms like Microsoft Teams and Udemy, the program is accessible worldwide, blending live sessions with on-demand content.

Marketing strategies include digital outreach and showcasing success stories, like Chen's, who improved his business's productivity post-training. The hub continually adapts its content to stay current with AI developments, focusing on sector-specific applications of ChatGPT.

This case study shows how Customized ChatGPT Learning Hub successfully meets the diverse AI training needs, preparing individuals and businesses to maximize ChatGPT's potential.

This section will guide you through creating and offering tailored training programs that unlock the potential of ChatGPT for eager learners.

Step 1: Identifying Your Target Audience

To craft an effective training program, begin by pinpointing who you aim to teach. Conduct surveys or interviews to understand the needs of different demographics. Is your audience comprised of professionals looking to automate work tasks, writers seeking creative inspiration, or programmers aiming to integrate ChatGPT into their projects? Create audience personas to represent the typical learner profiles you aim to serve.

Step 2: Develop a Curriculum

Your curriculum is the backbone of your training program. Start with the basics: what is ChatGPT, how does it work, and what can it do? Gradually introduce more complex concepts and uses, such as customizing ChatGPT responses or integrating the AI into personal workflows. Every module should include clear learning objectives, step-by-step instructions, and real-world tasks encouraging learners to apply their new skills.

Consider using varied instructional materials, such as video tutorials, reading materials, and interactive quizzes.

Step 3: Setting Up Training Platforms

Choose a platform that aligns with your teaching style and your audience's learning preferences. Tools like Zoom or Microsoft Teams can facilitate live, interactive sessions for synchronous learning. Platforms like Teachable, Udemy, or YouTube can host your pre-recorded content for asynchronous learning. Ensure the platform supports the interactivity required for effective learning, such as Q&A features, discussion boards, and assignment submissions.

Step 4: Marketing Your Training Services

To attract learners, your marketing strategy must be multifaceted. Develop a content marketing plan that includes educational blog posts, AI tool reviews, and success stories. Utilize social media platforms—LinkedIn for professionals, Instagram for creatives, Twitter for quick updates—to share insights and snippets of your training content. Participate in online forums and groups related to AI and ChatGPT to showcase your expertise and offer valuable advice, subtly directing interested individuals to your training services.

Step 5: Conducting the Training Sessions

When conducting sessions, engagement is key. Start with ice-breaker activities related to AI to warm up the group. Incorporate a mix of lecture, discussion, demonstration, and hands-on practice. Use case studies to show how ChatGPT can be applied in various scenarios. Simulate real-life challenges and guide learners through the problem-solving process using ChatGPT. Record your sessions so learners can revisit the content and those in different time zones can engage with the material.

Step 6: Providing Post-Training Support

After the formal training sessions conclude, ongoing support cements the learning experience. Set up a dedicated online community, such as a

Slack channel or a Facebook group, where learners can share their progress, ask questions, and provide peer support. Offer office hours or schedule follow-up webinars to address more complex inquiries or to cover new updates in ChatGPT's evolution. This also opens the door for you to build an audience so you can sell more services and products in the future as you expand your offerings.

Conducting Corporate Training Workshops

Workshops are a dynamic way to introduce, educate, and implement AI technologies within companies and teams. They are particularly effective for detailed, hands-on learning and can lead to direct application and immediate results. This section provides a blueprint for organizing successful workshops in a corporate setting.

Preparation Phase

Identifying Workshop Goals: The first step in conducting a successful workshop is articulating clear objectives. What do you want to achieve by the end of the workshop? With ChatGPT, goals could range from enhancing customer interaction to streamlining internal communication. For instance, a seminar aimed at customer service teams might focus on leveraging ChatGPT to improve response times and personalize customer interactions. Consider providing workshops in an area of business in which you have professional experience.

Defining Target Audience and Scope: Understanding the audience is crucial for tailoring content. Assess the participants' familiarity with AI and ChatGPT and align the workshop scope with their needs and the organization's goals. The workshop might delve into technical integration for a team of engineers, while a marketing team might focus on using ChatGPT for content creation.

Developing Workshop Content: The curriculum should comprehensively introduce ChatGPT, its potential applications, and hands-on exercises. The content should progress logically, starting with basic concepts and building to more advanced implementations. Include case studies, best practices, and common pitfalls.

Logistics and Scheduling: Choose a conducive venue and schedule the workshop at a time that minimizes disruption to work. Ensure all necessary technology and materials are in place beforehand and that support staff is available to assist with any technical issues.

Execution Phase

Conducting the Workshop: Kick off the workshop with an overview of AI and ChatGPT, setting the stage for what's to come. Ensure the presentation is engaging and accessible, using layperson's terms when necessary to explain complex concepts.

Interactive Sessions and Live Demos: Incorporate live demos where participants can see ChatGPT in action. This could involve real-time interactions with the AI or demonstrations of how ChatGPT can be integrated into existing systems

Group Activities and Discussions: Facilitate breakout sessions where attendees can discuss how they might apply ChatGPT in their roles. Group activities encourage collaboration and help solidify learning through practical application.

Post-Workshop Phase

Follow-Up and Support: Provide attendees with resources such as guides, FAQs, and forums where they can continue learning and share experiences. Offer post-workshop support sessions to address any questions or challenges that arise.

Measuring Outcomes and Feedback: Establish key performance indicators to measure the workshop's effectiveness. Collect feedback from participants to understand what worked well and what could be improved in future seminars.

By following a structured approach from preparation to post-workshop support, you can help introduce AI technology to organizations while ensuring its successful integration and utilization for business enhancement. Through careful planning, execution, and follow-up, workshops can yield substantial benefits and transform operational efficiency.

Freelancing on Online Platforms

In the digital age, freelancing has emerged as a powerful avenue for professionals to offer their skills globally. With the advent of AI and machine learning, ChatGPT expertise is becoming a sought-after service. This section introduces strategies for identifying the best platforms for freelancers to offer ChatGPT skills and methods to market these services effectively to a global clientele.

Platform Selection Phase

Evaluating Freelance Marketplaces: Start by researching which online platforms are most receptive to AI-related services. Look for marketplaces with a strong technology orientation, like Upwork, Toptal, or GitHub Jobs, where there's a demand for AI expertise. Evaluate the clientele, project types, and payment structures of these platforms to determine the best fit for your skills.

Creating a Compelling Profile: Once you've chosen your platforms, create a profile that highlights your expertise with ChatGPT. Detail your experience, projects, and any relevant certifications. Be sure to articulate the value you can bring to potential clients with your ChatGPT skills.

Marketing and Outreach Phase

Defining Your Service Offerings: Clarify what services you offer related to ChatGPT. This could range from developing chatbots for customer service to integrating AI into content creation processes. Specify the problems you solve and the outcomes you enable for businesses.

Building a Portfolio: Develop a portfolio showcasing your work with ChatGPT. Include case studies, testimonials, and detailed descriptions of past projects. If possible, create a personal website or use portfolio features within the freelancing platforms.

Global Marketing Strategies: Leverage social media, professional networks, and content marketing to reach potential clients worldwide. Write articles or create videos that demonstrate your ChatGPT expertise and share insights into AI trends.

Networking and Partnerships: Engage with online communities related to AI and technology. Attend virtual webinars and participate in discussions to build your network. Consider partnerships with agencies that might need ChatGPT services for their clients.

Client Engagement Phase

Proposal Writing and Bidding: When applying for jobs, tailor your proposals to address the specific needs of the project. Highlight how your ChatGPT skills can solve the client's problems and contribute to their goals.

Client Communication: Maintain clear and professional communication with potential clients. Understand their needs, offer solutions, and be responsive to inquiries. Use video calls and collaborative tools to build rapport with international clients.

Delivering Quality Work: Ensure that you deliver high-quality work that meets the client's expectations. This will help build your reputation, leading to more referrals and repeat business.

Case Examples of Potential Clients

Small Business Owners: Small businesses might seek ChatGPT services to automate customer interactions on their websites or social media platforms. Demonstrate how ChatGPT can provide 24/7 support, helping them compete with larger companies.

E-Commerce Sites: Online retailers could use ChatGPT to enhance their customer service or to create product descriptions. Use case examples to show how ChatGPT can scale operations and improve the shopping experience.

Educational Institutions: Schools and universities may be interested in using ChatGPT for tutoring or administrative support. Showcase how ChatGPT can provide personalized learning experiences or streamline administrative tasks.

Content Creators and Marketers: These professionals could utilize ChatGPT for generating content ideas, drafting articles, or managing social media interactions. Provide examples of how ChatGPT can enhance creativity and engagement.

Freelancing on online platforms with a specialization in ChatGPT is a promising monetization strategy. By carefully selecting platforms, marketing your services effectively, and delivering value to a diverse range of clients, you can establish a successful freelance career in the burgeoning field of AI.

Consult for Businesses on Customer Support Automation

In an era where customer satisfaction is pivotal to the success of any enterprise, automating customer support with artificial intelligence stands as a beacon of transformation. As a ChatGPT implementation consultant, you are the vanguard, leading businesses through the intricate dance of integrating AI to enhance their customer support operations.

Note: This path requires more technical knowledge than just ChatGPT. This path is not for you if you don't aspire to a tech-focused career that includes programming knowledge and knowledge of other AI tools.

Step 1: Market Research and Identifying Potential Clients

Your journey begins in the trenches of market research. Dive deep into industries ripe for digital transformation—e-commerce, technology, services—and surface with a list of potential clients. Employ analytics to understand the volume and nature of customer interactions. Your goal is to identify businesses where ChatGPT can significantly reduce response times, streamline service, and optimize customer satisfaction. Document case studies of businesses beleaguered by support queries, then illuminate how ChatGPT's integration can be their beacon of hope.

Step 2: Crafting Your Value Proposition

With your market intelligence in hand, forge your value proposition. It must resonate with the pain points you've uncovered—speak to reducing response times, offering round-the-clock support, and sharpening the precision of automated responses. Your proposition should be a mirror reflecting how ChatGPT will transform their current reality into the customer support utopia they desire.

Imagine you've conducted thorough research and discovered that a mid-sized e-commerce company struggles with an overwhelming volume of customer inquiries, especially after hours, leading to delayed responses and frustrated customers. Your value proposition could be something like this:

"Empower your e-commerce business with a ChatGPT-driven support system that never sleeps. Our bespoke AI solutions are tailored to halve your response times, ensuring every customer receives instant, accurate assistance, any time of day. We specialize in refining ChatGPT's capabilities to understand and address your customers' needs with precision, transforming your support from a bottleneck to a business accelerator. With our expertise, watch your customer satisfaction soar as we turn your support into a 24/7 powerhouse, driving loyalty and sales."

In this value proposition, you're directly addressing their pain points—slow response times and limited after-hours support—by offering a solution that provides immediate, all-day customer service. You're not just selling a product; you're selling an outcome that the e-commerce company desperately needs.

Step 3: Engaging with Businesses

Here, the art of engagement converges with the science of strategy. Craft communication templates for LinkedIn, industry forums, and direct emails that articulate your value proposition with precision. Guide the reader on how to tailor these templates to each prospective client, making every pitch a personalized one.

Step 4: Conducting Needs Assessment

No two businesses are the same, and your needs assessment must be equally unique. Offer a robust framework for dissecting a client's customer support operation. This framework should empower the reader to pinpoint inefficiencies and tailor ChatGPT solutions that align with the client's specific needs. Equip them with the tools to measure current support metrics and forecast the post-ChatGPT environment.

Step 5: Tailoring ChatGPT Integration Solutions

Integration is not a one-size-fits-all solution. Discuss the technical intricacies of embedding ChatGPT into varying infrastructures. Whether it's as part of an existing CRM or a standalone application, elucidate how to ensure a seamless melding of tech. Offer guidelines for maintaining the client's brand voice within ChatGPT's responses and customizing the AI to cater to industry-specific vernacular.

Step 6: Implementation and Training

Implementation is where the theoretical becomes practical. Walk the reader through a meticulous deployment plan, emphasizing testing and feedback. Provide a comprehensive training module for the client's team, ensuring they are adept in managing and leveraging ChatGPT's capabilities. Stress the importance of establishing feedback loops for ongoing system refinement.

Step 7: Follow-up and Ongoing Support

The consultant's role doesn't end at implementation. Lay out a structured follow-up plan that ensures the AI system matures in tandem with the business. Instruct on how to quantify the long-term benefits of ChatGPT and communicate this effectively to the client. Offer strategies for identifying new consulting opportunities that arise as the business and its needs evolve.

Advancing Your Business Through Professional Growth

In the business of consulting, training, or freelancing with ChatGPT, establishing a solid foundation is just the beginning. To truly thrive, you need to continuously evolve and reinforce your brand. Professional development is a critical component in this evolution. By constructing a compelling portfolio, you demonstrate the tangible results of your expertise. Engaging with the community not only expands your network but also opens doors to collaborative ventures and insight into emerging trends. Meanwhile, obtaining specialized certifications not only validates your skills but also assures clients of your commitment to excellence. This section discusses how you can align these elements of professional development with your business goals, creating a synergistic effect that propels your ChatGPT enterprise to new heights.

Building a Portfolio

A professional portfolio serves as a tangible representation of your skills and achievements. For a ChatGPT expert, it is a curated collection of work that demonstrates expertise in AI and conversational design.

Components of a Strong Portfolio:

- **Project Summaries:** Brief overviews of projects you've completed, highlighting the challenge, your solution using ChatGPT, and the results.
- **Testimonials:** Positive feedback from clients or collaborators, emphasizing your skills and their satisfaction with your work.

- **Visual Evidence:** Screenshots, links, or demos of ChatGPT interfaces you've created or improved.
- **Reflections:** Personal insights on what you learned from each project and how you've grown professionally.

Tips for Compiling Your Portfolio:

- Select a variety of projects that showcase a range of skills and challenges.
- Include metrics or statistics that demonstrate the impact of your work.
- Update your portfolio regularly with new projects and testimonials.

Networking and Community

Building a network within the ChatGPT community can lead to new opportunities, partnerships, and insights into the evolving AI and language models environment.

Engagement Strategies:

- **Join Forums and Groups:** Participate in online forums, social media groups, and platforms like GitHub or Stack Overflow.
- **Attend Events:** Look for conferences, webinars, and meetups that focus on AI, machine learning, and natural language processing.
- **Contribute to Open Source Projects:** Engage with the community by contributing to open-source projects involving ChatGPT.
- **Share Knowledge:** Write blog posts, create tutorials, or present at events to share your expertise and experiences.

Benefits of Networking:

- Access to a broader range of job offers and collaborative projects.
- Increased visibility within the ChatGPT ecosystem.

- Opportunities for learning and professional development.

Certification and Credentials

In a field as specialized as AI, certifications can validate your expertise and distinguish you as a knowledgeable professional.

Sources for Certification:

- **Academic Institutions:** Look for courses and certificates offered by universities known for their AI programs.
- **Online Learning Platforms:** Platforms like Coursera, Udacity, or edX offer courses designed in collaboration with industry leaders.
- **Industry Certifications:** Seek out certifications from companies or organizations that are recognized in the field of AI and machine learning.

Maintaining Credibility:

- Stay updated with the latest developments in ChatGPT and AI technologies.
- Renew certifications as required and seek advanced credentials.
- Highlight your certifications in your portfolio, resume, and professional profiles

Prompt Engineering: A Career in Crafting Conversations

The role of a prompt engineer is emerging as a cornerstone of effective AI utilization. As businesses seek to harness the power of advanced language models like ChatGPT, the expertise of a prompt engineer becomes indispensable.

Prompt engineering is the art and science of designing inputs that elicit the desired outputs from AI language models. It is a discipline that demands a nuanced understanding of natural language processing and machine learning, as well as a flair for crafting prompts that guide AI to fulfill specific tasks with precision and human-like understanding.

A prompt engineer stands at the intersection of AI technology and human communication. Their primary responsibility is to develop prompts that maximize the efficiency and context-awareness of AI responses. This requires a deep understanding of the language model's capabilities and limitations, the context in which it operates, and the target audience it serves. Daily tasks may include iterative testing, prompt optimization, and outcome analysis to ensure that interactions are as fluid and productive as possible.

To thrive as a prompt engineer, one must possess a blend of technical and soft skills. A strong grasp of AI principles, familiarity with NLP techniques, and programming knowledge are foundational. Equally important are the soft skills: critical thinking to troubleshoot and iterate on prompts, excellent communication to explain complex concepts simply, and the creativity to see beyond conventional use cases and drive innovation.

In practice, prompt engineering can significantly enhance the user experience across various business functions. For instance, a well-crafted prompt can improve customer service interactions with chatbots, yielding quicker and more accurate responses. In content generation, it can lead to more relevant and engaging material. By strategically implementing prompt engineering, companies can ensure their AI systems operate at peak performance, delivering tangible business benefits.

Job Market and Opportunities

The demand for prompt engineers is growing, as more industries recognize the value of optimized AI interactions. Tech companies, customer service sectors, and businesses focusing on digital content are actively seeking professionals who can refine and enhance their AI applications. The role of a prompt engineer is becoming more prominent as companies strive to differentiate their AI capabilities in a competitive market.

Future of Prompt Engineering

The future of prompt engineering is as dynamic as the field of AI itself. Continuous learning in a critical component of career longevity. As AI models evolve, so too will the strategies and techniques required to interact with them effectively. Prompt engineers will need to stay abreast of AI trends and developments, ensuring they can adapt their skills as AI evolves.

Becoming a Prompt Engineer: A Streamlined Pathway

Forge your path to becoming a prompt engineer with a focused approach that combines self-learning, practical experience, and community engagement, all while managing costs effectively.

Educational Foundation

- **Computer Science Principles:** Utilize free online resources and MOOCs like Coursera, edX, or Khan Academy to learn the basics of computer science.
- **Linguistics Fundamentals:** Explore language structure and function through free online linguistics courses offered by universities or educational platforms.

Specialized Knowledge

- **Natural Language Processing:** Enroll in no-cost courses from providers like Fast.ai, which offers a practical deep learning course for coders.
- **Machine Learning:** Tap into Google's free Machine Learning Crash Course or Stanford University's free introductory course on ML.

Practical Skills and Tools

- **Open-Source Contributions:** Engage with open-source projects on platforms like GitHub to gain hands-on experience and collaborate with the community.
- **AI Platforms Practice:** Experiment with AI and ML tools using the free tiers of services like OpenAI's GPT-3.5 or TensorFlow's playground.

Portfolio and Real-World Experience

- **Showcase Projects:** Create a portfolio on GitHub to display your projects, documenting your progress and solutions.
- **Internships and Work Experience:** Seek volunteer opportunities or internships that allow you to work on real-life projects.

Continuous Learning and Networking

- **Certifications:** Earn free or low-cost certifications through platforms like Udacity or freeCodeCamp to validate your skills.
- **Community Engagement:** Join AI and ML forums, attend local meetups, and participate in online communities such as Stack Overflow or Reddit's r/MachineLearning.

Entering the Job Market

- **Job Search:** Leverage LinkedIn, Indeed, and AngelList for job opportunities, and filter for roles that value skills over formal education.
- **Career Advancement:** Once you're in the field, seek mentorship, and continue learning to progress your career.

By embracing free or affordable learning resources and practical experiences, you can build a career in prompt engineering without incurring significant educational expenses.

In conclusion, prompt engineering represents a cutting-edge career path for those who are passionate about AI and possess the right mix of technical and creative skills. It is a profession that not only offers intellectual satisfaction but also holds the promise of growth and opportunity in an AI-driven future.

Chapter Wrap-Up

Let's wrap up our exploration of turning your ChatGPT skills into profit. Imagine yourself as the go-to expert aiding businesses in integrating ChatGPT for engaging customer service, or envision hosting workshops where you unveil the magic of ChatGPT's capabilities. If freelancing is your style, it opens up a world where you can select from an array of intriguing, global projects tailored to your interests.

For those captivated by the expansive potential of AI, our adventure is just beginning. The next chapter will widen your perspective, introducing you to a spectrum of AI tools beyond ChatGPT. We're moving beyond practical applications to enrich your understanding of AI's broader impact and potential. This will be a purely informational dive, perfect for those excited to deepen their knowledge of the AI field without the immediate pressure of application. If you are interested in learning more about how to begin a lucrative career in AI, a bonus chapter later in the book discusses this. With that, let's keep charging forward.

Chapter 9

Beyond ChatGPT – A Tour of Diverse AI Tools

In previous chapters, we have explored ChatGPT, which you've likely come to realize by now is a remarkable AI-powered tool that has revolutionized the way we interact with technology using natural language. ChatGPT's ability to comprehend, generate, and engage in human-like text has set a new standard in the field of artificial intelligence. However, the world of artificial intelligence is full of innovative tools, and ChatGPT is just one of the many stars in this expansive universe.

In this chapter, we will expand our focus beyond ChatGPT and look at the broader spectrum of AI tools that are equally important and shaping the future in profound ways. Each tool is like a piece of a larger puzzle, working together to create a complete picture of what AI can offer. With specialized tools ranging from machine learning frameworks that can predict trends to NLP platforms that understand the nuances of human speech, the ecosystem is teeming with AI tools, each with its own strengths and potential applications.

The objective of this chapter is to provide you with a panoramic view of the AI tool ecosystem, helping you understand the capabilities, functions, and specific niches of various AI technologies. By the end of this chapter, you will have a more comprehensive understanding of the AI tools available to you. This knowledge will help you select the right tool for your needs, whether it is for business, personal projects, or sheer curiosity.

Let's begin!

The Expanding AI Tool Universe

Diving into the AI ecosystem reveals a diverse array of tools, each with a unique contribution to technological progress. This ecosystem is not solely about the tools themselves but their application across various domains: from parsing and generating human-like text to recognizing patterns in data, and from powering creative endeavors to streamlining repetitive tasks.

Within the sphere of Natural Language Processing (NLP), we encounter tools designed for understanding, processing, and replicating human language, revolutionizing our interaction with digital systems. NLP sits at the core of sophisticated chatbots and voice-operated services, allowing for more natural and intuitive communication.

Moving on to Machine Learning Platforms, these robust frameworks are the engines behind data-driven insights and predictive analytics. They serve as the foundational structures for algorithms that distill complex data into discernible patterns, facilitating intelligent decision-making and process automation.

The category of AI for Creativity showcases the adaptability of AI, with tools that assist in music composition, art generation, and other creative productions. These innovative applications challenge our traditional views of creativity, offering novel avenues for artistic expression.

Each category within the AI ecosystem plays a distinct role. Gaining an understanding of this environment is key to utilizing it to its full potential. Whether it's to advance a business process, enrich a creative venture, or forge a new AI application, the appropriate tools can unlock a wealth of new opportunities and drive us toward an advanced future. As we proceed, we'll delve into the functionalities of these tools, their capabilities, and their current and potential uses in forging paths to new discoveries.

Machine Learning Workhorses

In the toolkit of modern AI, TensorFlow and PyTorch stand as pivotal frameworks in machine learning. These powerful libraries are essential for anyone looking to harness the capabilities of AI for data-driven problem solving and innovation.

TensorFlow, developed by the Google Brain team, is renowned for its flexible architecture that allows for easy deployment across a variety of platforms, from servers to edge devices. Whether you're developing models that predict consumer behavior or creating systems that can diagnose medical images, TensorFlow provides the robust, scalable infrastructure needed to bring these complex models to life.

PyTorch, with its dynamic computation graphs and efficient memory usage, is favored by researchers and developers who require flexibility and speed in model experimentation and prototyping. It shines in environments where rapid testing and iterative adjustments are key, such as in the development of autonomous vehicles or in the fine-tuning of language models.

When comparing TensorFlow and PyTorch, it's important to consider your project's specific requirements. TensorFlow is often lauded for its production-ready environment and extensive community support, making it a solid choice for deploying machine learning models at scale. PyTorch, on the other hand, is celebrated for its intuitive interface and ease of use, particularly useful for those in the research phase or when time to market is less of a concern.

Choosing the right tool depends on several factors: the scope and scale of your project, the need for rapid prototyping versus long-term stability, and the resources available to you for development and deployment.

Natural Language Processing Platforms

Natural Language Processing, or NLP, stands as a pillar of AI, giving machines the ability to interpret and generate human language. In this section, we examine two major NLP platforms: IBM Watson and Google's BERT, each bringing a set of powerful tools to the table.

IBM Watson has carved out a niche for itself with its robust capabilities in understanding and processing natural language. Its suite of applications has been influential across sectors, assisting legal professionals in sifting through case files, helping doctors and nurses in healthcare to parse patient information, and aiding customer service agents in providing prompt responses. Watson's versatility in processing complex language structures makes it an indispensable tool for businesses looking to derive insights from unstructured data.

On the flip side, Google's BERT (Bidirectional Encoder Representations from Transformers) has had a seismic impact on how search engines understand the intent behind users' queries. By processing words in relation to all the other words in a sentence, rather than one-by-one in order, BERT can comprehend the full context of a word by looking at the words that come before and after it. This has significant implications for search algorithms and data processing, making it easier for machines to understand the nuances of human language.

When examining IBM Watson and Google's BERT, it's evident that while both are designed to tackle the complexities of human language, they serve different functions. Watson is often implemented as an end-to-end solution for business applications, whereas BERT is primarily used to enhance the understanding and relevance of search algorithms.

Selecting between these platforms for your NLP needs involves a consideration of your specific objectives. Are you looking to deploy an AI system that interacts with customers and needs to understand the subtleties of human emotions and expressions? IBM Watson might be your pick. Or are you working to improve how information is retrieved and classified, ensuring that the context is fully captured? Then BERT could be the optimal choice.

Creative AI – From Art to Music

AI is not just a tool for analytical tasks but is also an emerging partner in creative industries, offering novel ways to harness creativity and influence the arts. Whether you're an artist, musician, or simply an enthusiast of the creative arts, understanding the capabilities of AI in these fields is pivotal for staying connected to the pulse of innovation in art and entertainment. AI tools like DALL-E and Jukebox are at the forefront of this innovative surge, pushing the boundaries of how we create and interact with art and music.

DALL-E, an AI program by OpenAI and accessible through a ChatGPT paid subscription, is reshaping the process of image creation. With the ability to generate detailed visuals from textual descriptions, this tool opens up new avenues for artists and designers, combining their creative visions with the algorithm's generative capabilities. This fusion of human imagination with machine precision allows for the creation of artwork that was previously inconceivable. Midjourney also does this same thing.

Similarly, Jukebox is redefining music generation. Developed by the same minds behind DALL-E, this tool can compose music in various styles, from classical to contemporary pop, creating novel melodies and harmonies that resonate with human emotion. The impact of Jukebox extends beyond just notes and chords; it's about understanding the essence of music composition.

The influence of creative AI on art and entertainment is profound. These tools not only provide new mediums for artists to express their creativity but also challenge our traditional understanding of the creative process itself. They serve as collaborators in the artistic journey, offering infinite possibilities for innovation and expression.

103

AI in Data Analytics and Business Intelligence

The surge of AI integration into data analytics and business intelligence is revolutionizing how organizations derive insights from their data. Tools such as DataRobot and Tableau's Einstein Discovery are at the helm of this transformation.

DataRobot stands out by automating the machine learning process, enabling users to build predictive models with unprecedented speed and efficiency. It democratizes data science by allowing those without a deep background in the field to create models that inform decision-making processes. For businesses, this means faster insights and the ability to act on data-driven strategies more quickly.

Tableau's Einstein Discovery, on the other hand, brings AI-driven analysis directly into the business intelligence environment. It seamlessly integrates with Tableau's interactive visual interface, making complex data more understandable and actionable for decision-makers. With the power to identify patterns and predict outcomes, Einstein Discovery is a tool that not only informs but also empowers users to take proactive measures based on solid data insights.

The impact of AI in this sector is multi-faceted. It not only automates mundane tasks but also enhances the accuracy of forecasts and provides a deeper understanding of market trends and consumer behavior. As we discuss these tools, you'll see how AI in data analytics and business intelligence is not just about processing information but also about unlocking the hidden value in data, enabling smarter decisions that drive business growth.

Conversational AI and Virtual Assistants

ChatGPT isn't the only Conversational AI tool on the market. The field of Conversational AI and Virtual Assistants is a bustling hub of innovation, where platforms like Azure Bot Service, Amazon Lex, and DialogFlow are key players, each providing unique functionalities for creating virtual conversational agents.

Azure Bot Service is a comprehensive framework that supports a wide array of conversational capabilities, enabling developers to build, test, and deploy bots across multiple channels. Its integration with Microsoft's cognitive services allows for sophisticated interactions, making it suitable for enterprises looking to implement robust conversational agents.

Amazon Lex, which powers Amazon Alexa, offers deep learning functionalities that enable developers to create bots with lifelike conversational interfaces. Its speech recognition and natural language understanding capabilities make it a strong contender for voice-driven applications and chatbot solutions.

DialogFlow, backed by Google's machine learning expertise, excels in creating interfaces that engage users with natural and dynamic dialogue. It stands out with its support for multiple languages and seamless integration with Google's ecosystem, making it ideal for those looking to globalize their chatbot services.

When implementing conversational AI, the choice between these platforms hinges on several factors. Azure Bot Service is often favored for its enterprise-grade integration, Amazon Lex for its voice services, and DialogFlow for its multilingual support and ease of use.

Best practices in deploying conversational AI involve understanding the specific needs of your user base, the context in which the bots will operate, and ensuring that the dialogue flows as naturally as possible. Additionally, it's important to continuously test and refine your bots based on user feedback and interactions to improve accuracy and user satisfaction.

Robotics and Automation

The synergy between robotics and artificial intelligence has given rise to a new era of efficiency and innovation, particularly through Robotic Process Automation (RPA) tools such as UiPath and Blue Prism.

UiPath is a leading RPA tool that empowers organizations to automate routine desktop tasks. Its drag-and-drop interface allows users to design automation processes visually, without the need for complex coding. This makes UiPath a favorite among companies seeking to streamline their operations and reduce manual workload.

Blue Prism, another frontrunner in the RPA space, offers a more enterprise-centric approach. It is known for its secure and scalable platform, which enables businesses to automate a broad spectrum of processes, enhancing accuracy and efficiency. Blue Prism's robust architecture is particularly well-suited for large-scale deployments that require strict governance and compliance.

AI's intersection with robotics has significantly altered how physical tasks are approached and executed. These intelligent automation tools are not just completing tasks; they're learning and adapting, thereby changing the operational fabric of industries. They're designed to handle repetitive tasks, allowing human workers to focus on more strategic and creative endeavors.

By integrating these tools, organizations can enjoy a dual benefit: the meticulous precision of robots, coupled with the cognitive understanding of AI. This section will offer you a glimpse into how RPA tools like UiPath and Blue Prism function and the transformative effects they can have on workflows and productivity. Whether you're looking to automate data entry, customer service inquiries, or any other repetitive task, RPA tools provide a pathway to a more automated, efficient, and error-free operation.

Ethical AI and Governance Platforms

The integration of ethics into AI development is not just crucial; it's imperative for the sustainable advancement of technology. Platforms like Salesforce's Einstein are leading the charge in ethical AI by providing tools that prioritize responsible AI practices.

Salesforce's Einstein platform embeds ethical considerations into the core of its AI applications, ensuring that decision-making algorithms are fair, accountable, and transparent. It provides businesses with the capability to manage AI deployments responsibly, allowing for the alignment of machine intelligence with human values.

Managing AI deployments extends beyond just functional outputs; it also involves maintaining clarity and transparency in how decisions are made. This means keeping stakeholders informed and involved in the AI's decision-making processes, ensuring that the AI's reasoning is understandable and its actions are in line with organizational ethics.

For those looking to integrate AI into their operations, understanding how to do so ethically will be a differentiating factor in the responsible application of these powerful technologies.

Implementing AI in Cloud Computing

The collaboration between artificial intelligence and cloud computing platforms has opened a new chapter in technological capabilities. Major cloud services like AWS, Google Cloud, and Azure have integrated AI tools that provide powerful, scalable solutions for businesses and individuals alike.

AWS, for instance, offers a suite of AI services that can enhance and automate complex tasks, from personalized recommendations to language translation. AWS's AI services are designed to be accessible to software developers at all levels, allowing them to infuse their applications with intelligent features without deep expertise in machine learning.

Google Cloud Platform also brings AI within reach through its AI and machine learning products. With services like AutoML and AI Platform, Google Cloud provides users with the tools to build and deploy machine learning models that are tailored to their specific needs, all hosted on Google's dynamic infrastructure.

Azure's AI services encompass a range of machine learning tools, knowledge mining, and cognitive services that can comprehend speech, make decisions, and analyze visual content. Azure makes it simple for developers to incorporate intelligent capabilities into their apps, with an emphasis on both user-friendliness and advanced analytics.

Each of these cloud platforms offers unique services that cater to the needs of different AI applications. Leveraging cloud AI for scalability means that as your demand for AI processing grows, these platforms can dynamically adjust to provide the necessary computational power.

Whether you're a startup looking to implement advanced AI on a budget or an established enterprise aiming to scale up your AI operations, cloud platforms offer the flexibility and power to meet your demands.

Customization and Specialization

As artificial intelligence continues to advance, a suite of niche AI tools has emerged, each designed to meet the specialized needs of different sectors such as healthcare, finance, and legal. These tools offer tailored solutions that address the unique challenges and requirements of each industry.

In healthcare, AI tools like Atomwise use algorithms to aid in drug discovery, while in finance, platforms such as Kensho analyze financial reports to predict market movements. The legal field also benefits from AI with tools like ROSS, which sifts through legal documents to assist in research.

Identifying the right AI tool for a sector-specific task involves a clear understanding of the unique problems and processes within that industry. It requires an assessment of how AI can improve efficiency, accuracy, and outcomes. For example, in healthcare, the priority may be on accuracy and compliance, while in finance, speed and predictive analytics could be more critical.

Utilizing specialized AI tools effectively demands a strategic approach. One must consider the integration with existing systems, the learning curve for users, and the scalability as industry demands grow. Whether streamlining complex tasks or unlocking new capabilities, specialized AI tools can provide a significant competitive edge in any industry.

Chapter Wrap-Up

As we draw this chapter to a close, we've navigated through an impressive array of AI tools, each with the potential to significantly influence and enhance various sectors. From the machine learning prowess of TensorFlow and PyTorch to the nuanced language processing of IBM Watson and BERT, and the inventive applications of DALL-E and Jukebox, we've seen how these tools can shape our approach to complex problems and creative endeavors.

We've also examined the intersection of AI with data analytics, business intelligence, and the critical role of ethical frameworks in AI development. Cloud computing platforms like AWS, Google Cloud, and Azure have been highlighted for their ability to scale AI solutions, while specialized tools have demonstrated their capacity to address specific industry challenges.

As you continue with AI, let the insights from this chapter serve as a foundation for your ongoing learning and experimentation. The field of AI is dynamic, with new tools and technologies emerging regularly. Staying current with these developments is not just a pursuit of knowledge—it's an investment in your future capabilities and success.

Consider this a gentle nudge to engage with the AI tools we've discussed. It's one thing to read about their capabilities, but the true depth of understanding comes from hands-on experience. Delve into TensorFlow or PyTorch and start a project, perhaps one that predicts customer behavior or identifies trends within your data. Use IBM Watson to analyze text or Google's BERT to refine your search capabilities. Create with DALL-E, compose with Jukebox, or implement an RPA bot using UiPath or Blue Prism.

And remember, the journey in AI is one best shared. Join online communities and forums where you can exchange ideas, seek guidance, and find inspiration. Places like Stack Overflow, Reddit's r/MachineLearning, or dedicated Slack channels are rich with individuals who share your interests and can offer support.

Take these steps, participate actively, and you'll find that the path to mastering AI is as rewarding as it is enlightening. The future of AI is being written by those who dare to apply their knowledge and share their discoveries. You can be one of those shaping what's to come.

Chapter 10

Keeping Up with the Speed of AI

Change is the only constant in the world of artificial intelligence. As we go through this chapter, it becomes clear that keeping up with the latest developments in AI is not a choice, but a necessity. To remain at the forefront, you must do more than just adapt to the fast pace of change in this field.

This chapter is your guide to staying relevant in the rapidly evolving field of AI. It presents proven methods for keeping up with the latest advancements while helping you stay ahead. In the world of new technologies and evolving ideas, it's important to remember that learning about AI is a continuous process. To stay ahead in this rapidly changing world, you need to keep learning new things.

Riding the Wave: Navigating the Changing World of ChatGPT and AI

The world is rapidly embracing AI, and according to Gartner, the use of AI has grown by a staggering 270% in just four years. This unprecedented growth is also reflected in the significant increase in AI-related patents, indicating many new ideas that are changing how technology is used, as reported by MIT Technology Review.

To keep up with these developments, there are various ways to stay informed about the latest trends and breakthroughs in AI. OpenAI's blog provides valuable insights into the AI world, sharing new developments and research results. Tech news websites such as VentureBeat, TechCrunch, and Wired are also essential platforms that offer perspectives on the most recent news and advancements in artificial intelligence. Reading such websites can help you stay informed about the latest happenings in the field.

But keeping up to date requires more than passively taking in information; it requires active participation. Continue reading research papers regularly to stay current on the latest AI research. Another option is to attend AI conferences and take advantage of the lively discussions there. These channels not only give you a deep look into the complexities of AI progress but also make it easier for people in the active AI community to connect and work together.

Knowing that AI is a dynamic, changing field is essential for people who are always trying to stay current. As we ride the crests and troughs of technological change, it's important to remember that keeping ahead of the curve in artificial intelligence is not just an admirable goal; it's the only way to ride the waves of innovation successfully.

Doing Your Research

In this section, we will discuss how engaging with AI thought leaders on social media, participating in AI forums, and expanding your professional network can significantly enhance your understanding and involvement in the field of artificial intelligence. By actively connecting with experts and communities online, you can stay up-to-date with the latest AI trends, gain valuable insights, and build meaningful professional relationships. These strategies can empower you to remain at the forefront of AI innovation and foster your growth in this exciting domain. Let's dive into how you can implement these strategies to keep yourself updated and grow your career in artificial intelligence.

Using Social Media to Follow Thought Leaders

In today's fast-paced world of AI innovation, it's not enough to just sit back and absorb new information. Thanks to the emergence of AI thought leaders and influencers, social media platforms like Twitter and LinkedIn have become vibrant places to get brief updates. You can customize your feed to receive real-time information that interests you. If you're looking to stay on the forefront of AI, consider following Dr. Fei-Fei Li, a renowned AI researcher and co-director of Stanford's Human-Centered AI Institute (Stanford Profiles, n.d.). These thought leaders serve as beacons that guide you in the right direction as AI advancements continue to evolve.

Signing up for AI Forums

When you become part of AI communities, you can experience the power of shared knowledge. Platforms like Stack Overflow and Reddit's r/MachineLearning are bustling hubs for both AI enthusiasts and professionals. These forums are not merely repositories of knowledge; they are living, breathing communities where people ask questions, share experiences and knowledge, and the collective wisdom grows. Being a part of these groups is not just about gaining knowledge passively; it leads to personal and communal growth. With a vast amount of information available on AI, such forums are excellent resources to stay up-to-date, ask questions, and learn from the experiences of others.

Developing Your Professional Network

Participating in AI platform communities is an excellent way to learn new things and expand your professional network. When you work in a team-oriented field, finding like-minded individuals with similar interests can help you feel more connected and motivated. The connections made in these online communities can extend beyond the realm of digital technology, creating a network of experts who not only share information but also contribute to the collaborative spirit that characterizes the AI community.

Evaluating the Information

Navigating through the endless amount of information available on AI and ChatGPT can be challenging. It is crucial to distinguish reliable and useful information from unreliable sources.

Access to information is a double-edged sword because not every piece of data is the same. While it can give you a lot of helpful information, it can also lead to wrong or out-of-date information. To ensure that you have reliable information, it is important to cross-reference from several trustworthy sites. This method can help you accurately and precisely navigate through the sea of information, ensuring that you reach your destination with the right information.

The main lesson to learn from this topic is to be cautious of information from unreliable sources. For instance, you must be careful while reading a blog post on an untrustworthy website that claims ChatGPT is excellent at forecasting stock market trends. We should not believe such claims blindly, as they can lead to poor decisions. Recognizing and avoiding false information is essential today, as fake news spreads at the same pace as the truth.

As AI and ChatGPT enthusiasts, it's essential to keep an open mind while simultaneously practicing healthy skepticism. The industry is continuously evolving, so it's crucial to be receptive to fresh perspectives and methods. While being open-minded is good, it's also important to be skeptical of new ideas' practicality and realism. A healthy balance of openness and critical thinking helps people stay informed and sort through the noise to find accurate information.

ChatGPT's New Features and Updates: Keeping Up with the Times

As AI is rapidly advancing, it is essential to anticipate and adapt to ChatGPT's new technological developments. To stay up-to-date and take advantage of each new development, this section offers a structured plan for adopting new technologies.

Learning About the New Features

ChatGPT evolves and gains new functionalities over time. To start exploring each update, it is crucial to understand how it works. OpenAI offers comprehensive documentation for every new feature they introduce. This documentation serves as a detailed roadmap, highlighting the latest tools available in the ChatGPT toolkit and how developers can utilize them. Anyone interested in learning more about the new features and enhancements in each update can leverage this material as a starting point.

Taking Notes on New Releases and Updates

OpenAI's release of ChatGPT-3 was more than just a model. It also came with a comprehensive guide showcasing the tool's new features. This launch exemplifies how proactive OpenAI is in constantly adding new features and ensuring users understand how to use them to their full potential. It's no longer simply a chore but an exciting opportunity to explore the uncharted territory of AI innovation as we consider the real-world implications of each new upgrade.

Playground Experiments

Experiment with new features by testing them out in a safe manner. By using a sandbox or working on a small-scale project, users can understand how each enhancement will impact them in the actual world. This testing phase enables users to learn about the subtleties, strengths, and potential weaknesses of new features before utilizing them in more extensive and critical projects.

Integrating Piece by Piece into Bigger Projects

It is strategically beneficial to add new features in stages. By doing so, users can incorporate them into more substantial and complex projects with confidence once testing confirms their viability in real-world scenarios. This gradual implementation approach minimizes the risk of using features that have not yet been tested in the field. It guarantees a seamless update process, enabling users to make the most of each feature without compromising the quality of their work.

The Future of ChatGPT: Looking Beyond the Horizon

True expertise lies in anticipating and utilizing tools like ChatGPT that will prove useful in the future. This section provides a guide on how to navigate unexplored territories of upcoming developments to ensure that users not only keep pace with the current wave of innovation but also move forward proactively and strategically toward the future.

An Eye on Emerging Trends

Although it is important to navigate the current state of AI, it is equally essential to look ahead and anticipate new trends. The rising popularity of quantum computing is a prime example of a potential force that could completely transform the field of AI, including ChatGPT. Quantum computing has the potential to exponentially increase computing power, leading to a new level of efficiency and complexity that has never been seen before. It is not only interesting to consider these emerging trends, but it is also vital from a business perspective. Being aware of these trends allows users to adapt and take advantage of the many opportunities that lie ahead.

Exploring Uncharted Territory

It's important to reflect on how new technologies can offer new opportunities by considering your current use. Regular self-reflection can guide you to think deeply about how you use ChatGPT and imagine how new features might lead you to uncharted areas. For example, if a future version of ChatGPT can understand and generate speech, you are encouraged to think about how you could use this skill professionally and personally. This introspective approach can empower you to be more than just a passive observer of progress. You can take charge of your AI learning trajectory and meaningfully shape its direction.

By following these strategies, users can ensure that their knowledge of ChatGPT is always up-to-date and adaptable. To stay ahead of the game, it's important to not only benefit from the latest advancements but also anticipate and prepare for the endless possibilities that lie ahead. This plan ensures that users don't just witness the evolution of AI over time; they actively engage and utilize ChatGPT's features to have the greatest impact possible.

Preparing for the Future with AI Education and Research

This section will focus on the platforms and resources that can enhance your knowledge and keep you informed about the latest in AI education and research.

Online learning platforms such as Coursera, edX, and fast.ai offer a range of courses and specializations that cover the breadth and depth of AI. These platforms collaborate with universities and industry leaders to provide up-to-date content that ranges from introductory courses in AI to advanced machine learning techniques. Whether you're a novice looking to understand the basics or a professional aiming to refine your skills, these platforms can be pivotal in your education.

Apart from structured courses, staying abreast of AI research and development is equally important. Resources like arXiv and Google Scholar allow you to access the latest research papers and findings in the field of AI. Journals such as "The Journal of Artificial Intelligence Research" and conferences like NeurIPS publish cutting-edge work that can provide deeper insights into where the field is headed.

Don't forget that communities and forums such as Reddit's r/MachineLearning, Stack Overflow, and GitHub provide spaces where you can engage with peers, discuss new findings, and contribute to open-source AI projects. These interactions are invaluable for practical learning and staying attuned to the pulse of AI progress.

By taking advantage of these resources, you can ensure that you are well-prepared for the future of AI, equipped with the knowledge and skills needed to navigate and contribute to this growing field.

Chapter Wrap-Up

As we come to the end of this chapter, we have explored the essential practices and mindsets needed to stay up-to-date in the field of artificial intelligence. Remember, adapting to the continuous changes in AI is not just a strategy, but a necessity for those who aspire to lead or innovate in this field. This guide has equipped you with the necessary tools to not only keep up but excel, highlighting the significance of continuous learning and flexibility. Remember, the field of AI offers endless opportunities for growth and discovery. As you move forward, carry the insights and strategies from this chapter with you to remain adaptable, informed, and always one step ahead.

Chapter 11
Navigating the Future with ChatGPT

In a few years, artificial intelligence virtual assistants will be as common as the smartphone. -Dave Waters

ChatGPT's journey into the future is more than just a glimpse into technological advancements. It goes deeper into the complex interactions between humans and machines. Initially, ChatGPT was a basic text model, but it has evolved into a sophisticated language model that can understand and produce natural-sounding text in various contexts.

ChatGPT has progressed beyond just responding to commands; it has developed the ability to comprehend context, imitate the subtleties of human speech, and adapt to the ever-changing nature of language. This evolution mirrors how communication becomes more intricate over time in real-life situations.

As we continue, it's important to note that ChatGPT's future is not predetermined. It's in constant flux due to advancements in AI and machine learning and the changing needs of its users. ChatGPT's disruptive potential extends beyond the boundaries of its code, affecting various areas such as private conversations among individuals, education, healthcare, and business.

Taking Advantage of the ChatGPT Wave of Progress

As an innovative pioneer in artificial intelligence, ChatGPT is continuously advancing with the latest innovations. OpenAI's commitment to improving ChatGPT is apparent in the significant improvements made to it regularly. The rapid transformation of ChatGPT-2 to ChatGPT-3 demonstrates how fast this technology is advancing. The model's ability to generate coherent and contextually appropriate text has taken a significant leap forward. ChatGPT-3 has demonstrated a quantum increase in context knowledge and a sophisticated understanding of various themes, which has improved the user experience. As of now, the model has advanced even further to ChatGPT-4. This upward trend highlights the importance of keeping up-to-date with ChatGPT developments.

Keeping up with these developments is more than just an academic interest; it has real-world implications for user experience. Those who use ChatGPT will be among the first to benefit from new updates and features as they become available. ChatGPT users can now realize its full potential with the seamless integration of state-of-the-art features into the platform in real-time, significantly expanding its possible applications.

Furthermore, users who are up-to-date on the latest developments are better equipped to resolve issues. Due to ChatGPT's iterative nature, its behavior may change slightly with each update. For example, a new ChatGPT version may modify how it responds to specific commands. Users can enhance the efficiency and effectiveness of their interactions with the model by staying informed of any developments that may impact their chosen prompt design. ChatGPT's flexibility significantly improves its usefulness, especially in dynamic settings where user requirements and expectations are continually evolving.

ChatGPT is set to become even more user-friendly, with more intuitive user interfaces on the horizon. As AI increasingly permeates everyday life, how we interact with it is also likely to undergo significant development. Given OpenAI's mission to make AI accessible to everyone, future iterations of ChatGPT may feature more user-friendly interfaces, straightforward installation processes, and comprehensive how-to documentation.

The trend towards user-friendliness is not just a nice-to-have; it is also a smart move to make AI more accessible to more people. By simplifying its interface, ChatGPT could benefit more people, regardless of their level of technical expertise. OpenAI's goal is to make AI accessible to as many people as possible, and this move towards greater openness aligns with that objective.

ChatGPT's Impact on Society

It's evident that ChatGPT possesses the capability to bring about significant change in various industries and leave a profound impact on society. Apart from facilitating communication between individuals, ChatGPT's potential extends to multiple domains, such as education and customer service (as discussed in previous chapters), leading to discussions about the future of work and raising complex ethical dilemmas.

Education

ChatGPT has the potential to revolutionize the way we teach and learn. This model is capable of generating text that is coherent and relevant to the context, which makes it a valuable tool for both educators and students to use in various educational settings. ChatGPT can usher in a new era of flexible and adaptable education by enabling the creation of personalized learning materials and providing instant access to tutoring services.

Eventually, students from all backgrounds and corners of the world can connect with an AI-powered tutor that caters to their specific learning needs. This feature can greatly democratize education by removing barriers and creating a more equitable and inclusive classroom environment for all students.

Changing the Face of Industry and Customer Service

ChatGPT technology has a broad range of applications beyond academic settings and can significantly improve customer service, among other areas. It can enhance interactions between businesses and their customers, leading to more efficient and personalized service delivery. Companies can leverage the power of ChatGPT-powered automated responses and virtual assistants to streamline their customer support operations, freeing up human resources for more complex tasks that require emotional intelligence and advanced decision-making skills.

Ethical Considerations

As the use of ChatGPT becomes more widespread, it is likely that concerns about its morality will arise. There are many unanswered questions that arise when using AI models more frequently. Concerns about data privacy, permission, and potential misuse are central to these moral challenges. ChatGPT's interaction with user-generated data necessitates stringent measures to ensure users' privacy. Additionally, it can be difficult to ensure that people follow the rules when using ChatGPT and do not abuse it.

It is worth noting that the White House has invested $140 million and issued policy recommendations to investigate and tackle the ethical concerns raised by AI (The White House, 2023). Developers, researchers, politicians, industry leaders, and the general public all share the responsibility of navigating these ethical considerations. If we want ChatGPT to have a positive, responsible, and value-aligned impact on society, we must collaborate to establish ethical frameworks and principles.

Job Evolution

The ability of ChatGPT to bring change raises questions about the future of jobs. Like any new technology, incorporating ChatGPT into different fields could lead to the automation of some jobs. This might transform the employment environment as artificial intelligence systems start taking over previously human-performed repetitive and routine work.

However, ChatGPT's rapid growth could also create exciting new job opportunities. AI ethicists, who ensure that people use advanced AI tools like ChatGPT responsibly, may soon be in high demand. Such ethicists would be essential in guiding the development of AI in a manner that respects societal values and prevents unforeseen consequences.

Gearing up for ChatGPT's Future

Learning or enhancing one's ChatGPT skills is crucial in today's world, as it can lead to a plethora of exciting professional opportunities.

Some Staggering Facts

An article published in Computerworld on August 22, 2023, cites the growing need for workers with AI expertise, especially in the field of generative AI tools, as evidence of the industry's rapid transformation. According to Upwork, 49% of hiring managers plan to hire more independent talent and full-time workers owing to AI deployment plans, signifying a significant workforce transformation (Mearian, 2023).

According to Mearian (2023), the second quarter of that year saw an extraordinary growth in job postings and linked searches of over 1000%. Hiring managers are looking for cutting-edge expertise in artificial intelligence. The top 10 generative AI-related abilities they want to see on a resume include fundamentals like Large Language Model, Generative AI, Object Detection, and ChatGPT.

In particular, OpenAI's ChatGPT received more searches from businesses than any other generative AI-related phrase in the first half of 2023. We can see the influence of ChatGPT in the six-fold increase in the number of job ads that include the terms GPT or ChatGPT between May 2022 and May 2023 on the professional networking website LinkedIn (Mearian, 2023).

Businesses are turning their attention from specialized generative AI tools to a broader range of uses, such as AI content production, Azure OpenAI, and rapid engineering. Companies are expanding their knowledge of generative AI beyond the confines of specific tools like ChatGPT, marking a significant milestone in the evolution of this field.

Since November of 2022, the number of job advertisements in English that include GPT or ChatGPT has increased by a factor of 21 (Mearian, 2023), demonstrating the widespread interest in these tools. Businesses are committed to investigating the possibilities presented by rapidly developing AI technology, as seen by their recruiting practices and increased activities.

According to LinkedIn data, the rate at which users added AI talents to their profiles has doubled since ChatGPT was introduced (Mearian, 2023) due to the growing demand for such expertise, demonstrating an increased awareness of the importance of skill sets necessary to integrate AI technologies effectively.

Concerns about job loss notwithstanding, the rise in AI-related courses on platforms such as LinkedIn Learning offers workers chances to improve their skills and get certified.

ChatGPT as a Career Catalyst

As we've learned already in this chapter, ChatGPT is helpful for more than personal reasons; it could lead to new and exciting job opportunities. More and more companies are realizing the game-changing potential of ChatGPT and other AI tools, resulting in a rise in demand for experts who can effectively employ such systems.

People who learn ChatGPT now will be at the forefront of a rapidly growing industry. As more and more companies want to implement AI solutions, employees skilled in ChatGPT will be in high demand. ChatGPT abilities have a wide range of potential uses, from improving customer service to creating novel educational solutions to assisting with the ethical deployment of artificial intelligence. This expertise improves one's existing talents and opens up doors to new professional possibilities as technology develops.

Mastering ChatGPT takes time and effort, but it's not just a skill to have now; it's an investment in your job that will pay off in the future. Experts in ChatGPT have a leg up on the competition as AI becomes more pervasive in all aspects of business.

Chapter Wrap-Up

The concluding chapter, Chapter 11, sheds light on the exciting prospects that lie ahead with ChatGPT, emphasizing the transformative potential of this dynamic technology. As we move forward, the rapid advancements in ChatGPT promise not only to enhance our personal and professional interactions with AI but also to bring about significant societal changes. To make the most of the possibilities offered by ChatGPT, we need to stay informed and adaptable, continuously evolving our skills and anticipating its impact on society. By proactively engaging with these developments, we can shape a future where AI amplifies human potential, drives innovation, and upholds ethical standards. This is not just about keeping pace with technology but about steering it towards a future that reflects our shared values and aspirations.

Share Your ChatGPT Experience: Leave a Review

Now that you've learned the basics of ChatGPT and mastered prompts so you can leverage your new knowledge to increase your productivity and make more money, it's your turn to light the way for others. Your honest review on Amazon can point fellow beginners towards this essential guide, helping them embark on their own ChatGPT adventure.

Your voice matters. By sharing your experience, you help others realize the potential of ChatGPT in their personal and professional lives. You're not just reviewing a book but guiding someone toward transforming their skills and opportunities.

Thank you for contributing to the community of ChatGPT learners. Together, we're nurturing a culture of growth and innovation in the world of conversational AI.

Scan the QR code below to leave a review. It only takes 60 seconds!

Conclusion

As we come to the end of our comprehensive examination of the fascinating world of AI and the transformative features of ChatGPT, it is important to reflect on the significant insights that have emerged throughout the readings in this book. This phase has involved a deep analysis of the fundamentals of artificial intelligence and a focused review of the unique advantages of ChatGPT. The concluding section serves as a guide, leading you through the key elements we have discussed and encouraging you to continue along your path into the opportunities offered by AI, and specifically ChatGPT.

Importance of Artificial Intelligence and ChatGPT

Let's revisit the main ideas we have covered in our conversation so far. We talked about the significance and potential of AI, and how ChatGPT stands out with its unique capabilities. Although AI is no longer a new concept, it has become increasingly important in both personal and professional domains. ChatGPT is a prime example of conversational AI, offering a wide range of applications. It can enhance individual productivity and transform entire industries. Moreover, it is not just a tool, but a gateway to a new era of human-computer interaction.

Applications in the Real World for ChatGPT

The advanced AI technology has not only theoretical value but also profound practical implications in various sectors. We have witnessed how ChatGPT can revolutionize different industries. For example, in healthcare, it assists in patient care and medical research. In education, it provides personalized learning experiences and supports educators. Its impact on customer service is undeniable, with instant and accurate responses. Additionally, it has transformative potential in creative fields by aiding in content creation, demonstrating its versatility. This book aimed to highlight the multifaceted ways in which ChatGPT can be integrated into daily tasks and professional environments. It showcases its capability to enhance efficiency, foster innovation, and create new opportunities for growth and development.

Keeping Up with the Most Recent Developments

Staying up-to-date with the latest discoveries in AI is not a choice, but a necessity. We highlighted the importance of continuously educating oneself and adapting to changes in technology, especially when it comes to using ChatGPT. As ChatGPT has evolved from previous versions, it's crucial to keep up with advancements in the industry.

Earning a Living with Your ChatGPT Skills

As we review the different chapters, let's keep in mind the various ways to monetize your ChatGPT skills. Your proficiency in ChatGPT puts you at the forefront of a burgeoning industry. You can leverage this by providing consulting services, developing applications, or getting involved in AI-based initiatives. Companies are also looking to hire individuals skilled with ChatGPT. Those who possess knowledge of current technological trends and actively contribute to their advancement will thrive in the future.

Implementing What You've Learned

Knowledge is only valuable when it is put into action. Now that you have gained some insights into ChatGPT's potential, it's time to start using it. You can begin by incorporating ChatGPT into your writing process, experimenting with different writing prompts, and exploring its capabilities as they relate to your professional pursuits. You may even consider entering the field of artificial intelligence, which is full of opportunities for those who are eager to seize them.

Considerations of an Ethical Nature

When harnessing the power of AI and incorporating ChatGPT into your toolkit, it is essential to pause and reflect on the ethical implications of technological advancements. You should always keep in mind the moral consequences of your actions, and strive towards the development of ethical and responsible artificial intelligence. You must aim to ensure that the impact of AI is positive and equitable for everyone.

The Prospects for ChatGPT and AI in the Near Future

As we approach the end of this book, it's essential to envision a future that's full of opportunities. The field of human computer interaction is entering a new era, and ChatGPT is one of the first signs of this transformation. The road ahead is filled with potential for new discoveries, innovative ideas, and significant breakthroughs. You play a crucial role in this pivotal era of conversational AI, so approach this evolving field with confidence and a forward-thinking mindset.

Now that you have gained the knowledge from reading these pages, your journey is about to continue beyond these concluding lines. Take the next step by exploring specific websites, enrolling in courses to expand your knowledge, joining online groups to participate in conversations, or starting your projects using ChatGPT. The extent of your opportunities will depend on your enthusiasm and openness to new experiences.

Keep in mind that you're not merely an observer of the AI revolution; you're actively shaping its development. You've only just begun, and the future of artificial intelligence, with ChatGPT at the forefront, is eagerly awaiting your contributions. Embrace the challenges, celebrate the successes, and carry on with your exploration of the fascinating world of artificial intelligence. You are the one in charge of writing the next story.

Chapter 12

BONUS CHAPTER: Customize ChatGPT to Reach Your Goals

Ready to take your ChatGPT experience to the next level? This chapter delves into the art and science of customizing ChatGPT, enabling you to forge an AI that resonates with the intricacies of your endeavors.

Imagine an AI finely tuned to the rhythm of your business, the creativity of your projects, or the depth of your academic research. This vision is within reach, thanks to the sophisticated tools offered by OpenAI. The capability to fine-tune ChatGPT is not just an advantage; it's a gateway to endless possibilities for entrepreneurs, educators, and enthusiasts alike. You'll discover how to select and prepare your data, utilize the GPT builder for customization, and apply your tailored model to achieve tangible results. Moreover, you'll learn to wield this potent technology with responsibility and ethical consideration.

As we embark on this exploration, you'll gain both the knowledge and the practical skills to construct a GPT that truly embodies your vision.

OpenAI's introduction of customization tools into AI has been revolutionary, enabling users to fine-tune Generative Pre-trained Transformers (GPT) to their unique specifications. This process of fine-tuning adapts AI to perform with an understanding of specific domains, preferences, or tasks, making it invaluable across various applications.

By retraining the base GPT model on a dataset you curate—be it academic texts, creative works, or industry-specific documents—you empower the AI to produce content that aligns more accurately with your objectives. OpenAI has made this powerful capability accessible to a wide audience, removing the barriers to entry for leveraging AI in personalized and impactful ways.

A Content Creator's Quest to Niche Domination

Consider Kevin, a content creator specializing in sustainable living. Kevin sought to establish a unique voice in the crowded space of environmental blogging and social media. By fine-tuning ChatGPT with articles, blog posts, and research papers on sustainability, renewable energy, and eco-friendly practices, Kevin created a custom GPT model capable of generating insightful, accurate, and engaging content tailored to the niche audience of sustainability enthusiasts.

This custom model enabled Kevin to consistently produce high-quality, relevant content that resonated deeply with the target audience, significantly increasing engagement on the blog and social media platforms. It also streamlined the content creation process, allowing Kevin to focus on strategy and community building. Kevin's success illustrates the potential of customized GPT models to empower content creators to carve out distinctive spaces in competitive markets.

Personalizing Learning for a Child with Special Needs

In another scenario, Jamie, a parent of a child with autism, sought innovative ways to support their child's learning. Traditional educational materials often fail to capture the child's interest or accommodate their learning style. Jamie decided to fine-tune a ChatGPT model using a collection of the child's favorite stories, educational games, and subjects of interest, along with expert guidelines on educational strategies for children with autism.

The customized GPT model became a versatile tool for Jamie, generating engaging, personalized learning materials that catered to the child's interests and learning needs. It facilitated interactive storytelling, created custom quizzes, and even offered explanations in a way that was comprehensible and captivating for the child. This case highlights the transformative potential of customized AI in personal and non-commercial contexts, offering bespoke solutions that address specific challenges and enrich lives in meaningful ways.

These case studies underscore the versatility and potential of ChatGPT's customization tools, showcasing how they can be employed to achieve personal and professional objectives. Whether it's advancing a content business or enhancing individual learning experiences, the ability to build custom GPT models opens up a myriad of opportunities for innovation and personalization in the digital age. Let's dig into how you can build your own custom GPT tailored to help you meet your goals.

How to Build a Custom GPT

Let's break down the process of building your own GPT model into manageable steps.

1. Identifying Your Goals

First things first, let's chat about your endgame. What do you envision your custom GPT model doing for you? Think of this as setting up a GPS for your road trip – you need to know where you're heading. Are you looking to generate niche blog content, answer customer service inquiries, or compile code? Jot down the specifics. What tone should your AI embody? Professional, witty, or scholarly? Your data will need to reflect these traits.

2. Gathering and Preparing Your Data

Now, onto the fuel for your AI engine – data. Your custom GPT needs the right diet to perform well. Imagine you're crafting a recipe; the ingredients (your data) must be fresh and relevant. This means collecting text that's representative of the tasks you'll assign to your AI. Then, get your chef's hat on and prep it – format your data so it's clean and digestible for the GPT model. Think JSON files with clear labels, and keep an eye on OpenAI's data guidelines for best results.

3. Fine-Tuning with ChatGPT Builder

Ready to get your hands dirty? Let's roll up our sleeves and dive into the fine-tuning process. OpenAI's ChatGPT Builder is your workshop. Here's your toolkit:

- **Accessing the Builder**: Log into your OpenAI account and navigate to the fine-tuning section. Familiarize yourself with the interface.
- **Uploading Data**: Upload your prepped dataset. Ensure it's error-free – your AI is a sponge, it'll learn everything, warts and all.
- **Setting Parameters**: This is where you get technical. Set your training parameters – think of these like tuning an instrument for the perfect pitch. It'll determine how your model learns.
- **Kickstarting the Training**: Hit that 'Train' button and watch the magic happen. Your model is now learning, rehashing that data into something new and tailored.

4. Testing and Evaluating Your Custom Model

It's showtime! Put your model to the test. Does it sing in the tone you want? Does it falter on high notes (complex queries)? Testing is about giving your AI a pop quiz to see if it studied well. Evaluate the responses, make notes, and be ready to go back to the tuning board if needed. Iteration is key – even the best need practice.

5. OPTIONAL: Integrating Your Custom GPT into Applications

(This activity requires some programming knowledge or the desire to learn. If this isn't you, please skip this step.)

Congratulations! Your custom GPT model is trained and ready to go. Now, it's time to put it to work. Think of your GPT as a specialized employee who can handle specific tasks in your digital workspace. Here's how to make the introduction:

Understanding API Integration

Your GPT model operates through something called an API (Application Programming Interface). It's a set of rules that allows your applications to communicate with the GPT model. You can think of it like the way you place a food order at a restaurant; you give specifics, and the kitchen (in this case, the GPT model) prepares your order (the output).

Prerequisites

- **API Key**: OpenAI will provide you with a unique key when you create an account. Guard this key like a treasure; it's your pass to use your model.
- **Development Environment**: This can be any code editor you feel comfortable with. There are plenty of free options like Visual Studio Code or Atom.
- **Programming Basics**: You don't need to be a pro, but understanding the basics of a programming language, like Python, is necessary. You can do so in as little as a week by checking out our other book Python Programming for Beginners Made Easy.

Step-by-Step Guide

Set Up Your Environment:

- Install a code editor if you haven't already.
- Install Python, which is the language we'll use to talk to your GPT model.
- Set up a project folder where you'll keep your integration scripts.

Install Required Libraries:

- Open your code editor and open a terminal or command line.
- Type `pip install openai` to install the OpenAI library, which is a collection of code that makes it easier to talk to your GPT model.

Write Your Integration Script:

- Create a new Python file in your project folder. You might name it `gpt_integration.py`.
- At the top of this file, you'll import the openai library with the line `import openai`.
- Below that, you'll set your API key. OpenAI's documentation will show you how to do this securely.

Communicate with Your GPT Model:

- Now, write a function that takes a prompt (a question or statement you want your GPT to respond to) and sends it to the model.
- The function will then wait for the response and print it out or send it where it needs to go.

Test It Out:

- Run your script with a test prompt to see if you get a response.
- If something goes wrong, check your code for typos and ensure your API key is correctly set.

Connect to Your Application:

- If your GPT model is going to be a chatbot, for example, you'll write code to take user input and use that as the prompt for your function.
- Your script sends the prompt to the GPT model and then delivers the model's response back to the user.

Debug and Secure:

- Test your application thoroughly to find and fix any issues.
- Make sure your API key is never exposed to the public. Follow security best practices as outlined in OpenAI's documentation.

Integration might involve trial and error, and that's perfectly normal. Don't be afraid to ask for help on forums or from more experienced coder friends. And always refer to OpenAI's documentation, which is rich with examples and tips.

As you get comfortable with the basics, you can start exploring more advanced features like handling different types of inputs, managing more complex conversations, or integrating with other services and APIs.

Remember, every expert was once a beginner. With patience and practice, you'll have your custom GPT model integrated into your application, enhancing your digital life in ways you've only imagined.

Exercise: Build a Custom GPT

Using the step-by-step guidance above and the resources provided, build your own custom GPT.

Maintaining and Improving Your Model

Now that you've integrated your custom GPT into your application, this isn't the end. Your model is like a garden; it needs regular care and the occasional refresh to thrive. Here's how to keep your digital garden blooming:

Regular Monitoring

Why Monitor?

- **Performance**: You want to ensure your model is still providing relevant and accurate responses.

- **User Satisfaction**: It's crucial to know how users are reacting to your model. Are they getting the help they need?
- **Error Rates**: Keep an eye out for increased error rates or patterns of misunderstanding.

How to Monitor?

- Use logging to record interactions. This can help you understand how your model is being used and identify any recurring issues.
- Collect feedback directly from users through surveys or a feedback option within the application.
- Set up alerts for anomalies in performance metrics, like sudden spikes in error rates.

Retraining with New Data

When to Retrain?

- **Data Drift**: If the type of data the model is interacting with starts to change, it may be time to retrain.
- **New Features**: If you want your model to handle new topics or tasks, you'll need to teach it with new data.
- **Performance Drop**: If the model's performance starts declining, fresh data might be the revitalizer it needs.

How to Retrain?

- Collect new and relevant datasets that reflect current usage and new features you want to implement.
- Use the fine-tuning feature of your GPT model to update its knowledge with the new data.
- Remember to validate the model with a fresh set of test data to ensure the retraining has been effective.

Fine-Tuning Parameters

As you gather more data on how your model is performing, you might find that adjusting certain parameters, like the temperature (which affects randomness of responses) or max tokens (which controls the length of responses), can improve outcomes.

How to Adjust?

- Use A/B testing to compare the performance of the model with different parameter settings. This means setting up two versions of your model with different parameters to see which performs better.
- Gradually implement changes based on the results of your tests and user feedback.

Maintenance Checklist

- **Weekly**: Review logs and user feedback for quick fixes and minor tweaks.
- **Monthly**: Check performance metrics and compare against goals.
- **Quarterly**: Plan for a retraining session if needed, considering new data and user requirements.
- **Bi-Annually**: Conduct a comprehensive review of the model's parameters and consider more significant adjustments or retraining with a substantial new dataset.

The Continuous Cycle

Maintaining a custom GPT model is a continuous cycle of monitoring, improving, and adapting. By staying attentive to the model's performance and the needs of your users, you can ensure that your GPT model remains a valuable asset.

In the digital garden of your custom GPT model, maintenance is the key to growth and longevity. With diligent care, you can cultivate a tool that not only answers the needs of today but also evolves to meet the challenges of tomorrow.

Resources and Support

Embarking on the adventure of building your custom GPT model doesn't mean you have to go it alone. There's a wealth of resources and communities out there ready to support you on your journey. Whether you're stuck on a technical problem or looking for inspiration, here's where you can turn to:

Documentation

- **OpenAI Documentation**: This should be your first port of call. OpenAI provides extensive documentation covering everything from getting started to advanced usage.

Link: OpenAI API Documentation

- **Model-Specific Guides**: For each GPT model, there are usually dedicated guides that can help you understand the nuances and best practices for that particular version.

Link: OpenAI Model Guide

Community Forums

- **OpenAI Community Forum**: A place to discuss ideas, share work, and get help from other GPT users.

Link: OpenAI Community

- **Reddit**: Subreddits like r/MachineLearning and r/LanguageTechnology are great places to seek advice and discuss your projects.

Link: Reddit Machine Learning

• **Stack Overflow**: For coding-specific questions, there's no better place than Stack Overflow. Use the openai-gpt tag to find relevant discussions.

Link: Stack Overflow

Support Channels

- **OpenAI Support**: If you encounter issues with the API or service, reaching out to OpenAI support can help resolve your problems.
- **Contact**: OpenAI Support
- **GitHub Issues**: For bugs or issues related to specific software libraries or tools, the Issues section of the relevant GitHub repository is the place to go.
- **Link**: GitHub
- **Technical Blogs and Tutorials**: Websites like Towards Data Science offer a plethora of tutorials and case studies that can provide guidance and inspiration.
- **Link**: Towards Data Science

Social Media and Networking

- **LinkedIn Groups**: Professional groups on LinkedIn can be a good place to network and find others who are working on similar projects.
- **Twitter**: Following AI experts and organizations on Twitter can keep you updated with the latest news and insights in the field.

Remember, these resources are just a starting point. The field is always evolving, and staying engaged with these communities and resources will help you stay at the forefront of GPT model development.

Chapter Wrap-Up

And there you have it – a map to guide you through the exciting terrain of custom GPT model creation. From defining your goals to integrating your model into applications, and maintaining its relevance over time, you're now equipped with the knowledge to begin crafting your AI personal assistant.

Remember, a refined and robust GPT model is iterative and ongoing. Use the resources and support channels listed to refine your craft, troubleshoot issues, and keep learning. Engage with the community, contribute to discussions, and don't shy away from asking for help when you need it.

References

Admin. (2019, June 28). *36 Inspirational Quotes On Big Data, Machine Learning And Artificial Intelligence*. Data Semantics. https://datasemantics.co/36-inspirational-quotes-on-big-data-machine-learning-and-artificial-intelligence/

Costello, K. (2019, January 21). *Gartner Survey Shows 37 Percent of Organizations Have Implemented AI in Some Form*. Gartner. https://www.gartner.com/en/newsroom/press-releases/2019-01-21-gartner-survey-shows-37-percent-of-organizations-have

Deutscher, M. (2024). *OpenAI's annualized revenue reportedly tops $1.6B*. Silicon Angle. https://siliconangle.com/2024/01/01/openais-annualized-revenue-reportedly-tops-1-6b/

Kolmar, C. (2023, June 11). *23+ Artificial Intelligence And Job Loss Statistics [2023]: How Job Automation Impacts the Workforce – Zippia*. Zippia - the Career Expert. https://www.zippia.com/advice/ai-job-loss-statistics/#:~:text=Automation%20and%20AI%20will%20lift

Markoff, J. (2011, February 16). On "Jeopardy!" Watson Win Is All but Trivial. *The New York Times*. https://www.nytimes.com/2011/02/17/science/17jeopardy-watson.html

Marr, B. (2023, May 19). *A Short History Of ChatGPT: How We Got To Where We Are Today*. Forbes. https://www.forbes.com/sites/bernardmarr/2023/05/19/a-short-history-of-chatgpt-how-we-got-to-where-we-are-today/?sh=386b957f674f

Mearian, L. (2023, August 23). *The most in-demand AI skills — and how companies want to use them*. Computerworld. https://www.computerworld.com/article/3705095/the-most-in-demand-ai-skills-and-how-companies-want-to-use-them.html

OpenAI. (2024). ChatGPT-4 [Software]. Retrieved February 28, 2024, from https://openai.com/chatgpt

Pykes, K. (2023, November). *An Introduction to Using DALL-E 3: Tips, Examples, and Features*. Datacamp. https://www.datacamp.com/tutorial/an-introduction-to-dalle3

Rotman, D. (2019, February 15). *AI is reinventing the way we invent*. MIT Technology Review. https://www.technologyreview.com/2019/02/15/137023/ai-is-reinventing-the-way-we-invent/

Stanford Profiles. (n.d.). *Fei-Fei Li's Profile | Stanford Profiles*. Profiles.stanford.edu. https://profiles.stanford.edu/fei-fei-li

Statista. (n.d.). *Artificial Intelligence - Global | Statista Market Forecast*. Statista. https://www.statista.com/outlook/tmo/artificial-intelligence/worldwide

The White House. (2023, May 4). *FACT SHEET: Biden-Harris Administration Announces New Actions to Promote Responsible AI Innovation that Protects Americans' Rights and Safety*. The White House. https://www.whitehouse.gov/briefing-room/statements-releases/2023/05/04/fact-sheet-biden-harris-administration-announces-new-actions-to-promote-

References

responsible-ai-innovation-that-protects-americans-rights-and-safety/#:~:text=The%
20National%20Science%20Foundation%20is

"The document was reviewed for clarity and grammatical accuracy using Grammarly."

144

Appendix

How to Fix Common Setup Issues

Troubleshooting: Common ChatGPT Errors and Fixes

Think of troubleshooting as more than simply something you have to do; it's a talent that will serve you well in the broader world of digital problem-solving, not just in the context of ChatGPT setup. Look at every setback as a chance to get better at this. You'll discover that the whole experience becomes formative with its problems and answers, creating the framework for mastery beyond the initial configuration. Sometimes, accessing ChatGPT may become a hassle due to several errors. Here's a rundown of typical error prompts and how to troubleshoot them.

Login Error

You'll get this error message when there's a problem with your ChatGPT login or authentication. An incorrect password is one possible cause. Or it could be an issue with the connection when trying to log in. Here's how you can troubleshoot it:

• Make sure you typed in the correct login information.

• Make sure your internet link is stable while you're logging in.

• If the problem continues, change your password or get help from the platform's support.

Body Stream Error

It means there is a problem with how the person and ChatGPT are sending or receiving data. It could be because the network is too busy, data bits are losing or messing up, problems with the database server, or problems with the user's internet link.

How to Fix or Troubleshoot:

• Make sure your internet link is stable.

• Reload the page or close and reopen the program to start a new data stream.

• If the issue continues, it may be a problem on the server. Get help by contacting the platform's support

Network Error

If a network error occurs, your device may have temporarily lost connection to the ChatGPT servers. The cause of this problem could be anything from an unstable internet connection to server issues or routine maintenance. There are several steps you can take to fix this issue.

• Make sure your internet connection is fast and reliable first.

• You can see if any problems or maintenance are happening with the ChatGPT servers by visiting the platform's status page.

• If these troubleshooting procedures don't solve the issue, you can try contacting your internet service provider or the platform's support team.

If you follow these instructions, you should be able to reduce the frequency and severity of network problems when using ChatGPT.

Access Denied or Error 1020

This error appears when the user's request is acknowledged, but they are not allowed access for several reasons. IP blocking or limits could be to blame. The security settings might also be stopping you from getting in. Here are some things you can try to fix this:

• Check to see if your IP address is banned or blocked.

• Configure device or network security.

• If the problem continues, get help from the platform's support.

Too Many Requests or Error 429

The user has made too many requests in too short a time, as shown by this error. Requests made quickly and more than once in a short time could be a reason. The following are the steps to troubleshoot and fix the issue:

• Reduce the frequency of requests to work within the platform's constraints.

• Check the platform's instructions to see how many requests you can make simultaneously.

• Increase your plan's storage and bandwidth if you think you'll soon reach them.

Unfinished Responses

When ChatGPT can't make a full or logical answer, it sends an "unfinished response." A possible cause is entry prompts that need to be clarified or specific enough. It could also be that the model doesn't understand everything well enough. The following are the steps to troubleshoot and fix the issue:

• Change how you word your entry prompts and clarify them so ChatGPT can understand them better.

• Try out different variations to get answers that make more sense.

- If the problem continues, you might want to give more information or break down complicated questions.

These steps for troubleshooting should help you fix the problems listed. If the issue persists, you should contact the platform's support team for personalized help.

Further Guidance

Don't Panic

Setup challenges shouldn't be seen as impassable walls but rather as opportunities to gain insight along the way. First and foremost, take your time when trouble arises. Although the setup process may seem complicated, it is a controlled environment where every problem has an answer just waiting to be found. Maintain your composure, and you'll see that fixing problems isn't a roadblock but a stepping stone to mastery.

Simple Problems, Simple Solutions

We can usually find simple answers in unexpected places, especially regarding the most typical types of errors. If you're having difficulties with OpenAI, you can refer to the documentation for help. This documentation is a detailed reference that shows you how to fix the most common issues. Every error you go into is a clue that points you in the direction of a solution that's been well-documented. Instead of viewing troubleshooting as an insurmountable obstacle, consider it an exciting investigation in which the solution to each puzzle is a step closer to complete mastery.

Online Resources

The internet community is a shining example when it comes to knowledge that goes beyond what we can find in books. Sites like Stack Overflow can act as intangible resources where people can pool their knowledge to help each other. Troubleshooting isn't something you do alone; it's an experience shared with others in which your difficulties can be resolved by someone who's been through it already. Use internet forums and draw on a pool of knowledge that goes far beyond your problem-solving skills.

Challenges Drive Growth

Recognize that troubleshooting is not a detour but a vital part of the setup process. Problems you run into act as learning opportunities, transforming you from a setup newbie into a seasoned pro. The trip isn't just about getting where you want to go; it's also about developing skills to help you deal with problems effectively and creatively.

Also by ModernMind Publications

Check out our other books by scanning the QR code:

Made in the USA
Las Vegas, NV
01 November 2024

10869483R00089